BATTLE SCARS
FADE
BUT NEVER HEAL

BATTLE SCARS
FADE
BUT NEVER HEAL

SGT. JERRY R. GANDY

CITI OF
BOOKS

CITIOFBOOKS, INC.
3736 Eubank NE Suite A1
Albuquerque, NM 87111-3579
www.citiofbooks.com
Hotline: 1 (877) 389-2759
Fax: 1 (505) 930-7244

Ordering Information:
Quantity sales. Special discounts are available on quantity purchases by corporations, associations, and others. For details, contact the publisher at the address above.

Printed in the United States of America.

ISBN-13:   Softcover   978-1-960952-86-8
              eBook   978-1-960952-87-5

Library of Congress Control Number: 2023913567

TABLE OF CONTENTS

DEDICATION

I would like to dedicate this book to my beloved wife of fifty-two years. She has been the love of my life and is the one who completes me. Her name is Faye and she is more beautiful today than she was when I returned from Vietnam. There is no doubt that God put us together, and I thank him for that every day. She stood by me through some really bad times, and I don't think that I would have had the will power to keep going if she had not been by my side. She has blessed me with three beautiful and wonderful daughters. Their names are Pollyanna, Shellie, and Ashley. They are grown up now and all have successful lives. Faye has been the most graceful wife and mother that any family could hope to have.

I hope that this book will help my wife and daughters to understand me a little better. They have seen my good sides, as well as my bad sides. I still have an occasional nightmare, or period of depression, but I have been able to put most of it in the past. I am occasionally given the privilege of speaking to groups of young people and I am able to use some of my past experiences to keep their attention. I like to think of myself as a Christian motivational speaker for young people. God has been good to my family and me. Each of my family members has come to know Jesus, as their personal savior. What more can a man ask for?

CHAPTER 1

THE EARLY DAYS

My childhood years were fairly normal. I grew up in a small town in Mississippi, the younger of two boys. I made average grades in school, and was very popular among my school mates. As I entered my teen years, new problems began to develop. I was extremely small for my age. The other guys would pick on me and crack jokes about me. They called me things like; shorty, half-pint, and shrimp. These remarks embarrassed me and made me mad. This caused me to get into a lot of fights. Luckily, I was pretty good at fighting, so I was usually able to hold my own, with most of the fellows. The principal at my school seemed to shun on fighting, so I got to spend a lot of time with him. I had my own assigned chair, in the corner of his office.

I never cared very much about sports, so I spent most of my spare time working. My best friends lived on a farm next door, and their dad would pay me to do odd jobs. I started out making 50 cents per hour, and earned every penny of it. I didn't mind the hard work, because I got to spend time with my friends and we had a lot of fun. We did things like milk cows, hauling hay, and working in their chicken houses. These things weren't done the same way back then, as they are today. My family wasn't poor and I didn't have to work, but I enjoyed it. I always had spending money, even before I was old enough to need it. I can't remember when I actually started working, I was probably about eight years old. At least, when I was working, I didn't have time to get into trouble. Around the ninth grade, I started thinking about the Army. The Vietnam War was beginning to produce a lot of American casualties. My interest in the military heightened, as the next few years went by. I watched a lot of news reports and followed our involvement in the Vietnam War. The paratroopers really got my attention, and I knew that someday I would be one of them.

In the eleventh grade, I began to enter a new world. I grew rather fond of my next-door neighbor, and I asked her to go out on a date with me. She must have had a very weak moment, because she agreed and we started dating regularly. She was three years younger than me, but we were extremely compatible. I shared my dreams and desires, about the Army with her, and she seemed to understand.

About halfway through my senior year, I went home one day and informed my parents that I was going to drop out of school and join the Army. My parents thought that this was probably a phase that I was going through, so they didn't really worry about it. They told me that I should finish school, and then I would have plenty of time to decide what I wanted to do with the rest of my life. I went down to the local recruiting station and told them that I wanted to join the Army. When I told them that I was only seventeen years old, they explained to me that one of my parents would have to come down and sign forms, giving their parental permission, before I could be accepted into the military. I went home that afternoon, and asked my parents to sign for me. My mom bluntly refused, and my dad said that he would have to think about it. A few weeks later, my dad came to me and said that he would make me a deal. He explained to me that Mother would never sign the form, because she was afraid that I would be sent to Vietnam, and I would get killed. Dad said that he would sign for me, because he knew that I was going to go in anyway, as soon as I had my eighteenth birthday. He said, that in turn for his signature, I must agree to graduate from high school and stick around long enough to receive my diploma. One of my mother's dreams was to see both of her sons graduate. This would only mean a few more weeks in school, so we shook hands and sealed the deal.

I was officially in the Army, about two weeks prior to my graduating from high school. I only requested three things from the Army: that I be placed in an infantry unit, that I be sent to Vietnam, and that I could be a part of the Airborne program. The Sergeant said, there should not be a problem with any of those three requests, ha. They delayed my entering basic training, for a few weeks. I joined the Army, as an infantryman, with the option of becoming a real live paratrooper. I was walking on cloud nine. As my departure date got nearer and nearer, I began to have doubts about the decision that I had made. To be truthful, I was scared to death. I didn't share my feelings with anyone. I wanted everyone to forget my size, and look at me as a brave young man who was volunteering to serve his country, and possibly give his life for it.

Faye and I had really fallen for each other. We had even discussed marriage, but I knew that would be a dumb thing to do, at this point in our lives. I didn't think that it would be fair for me to put that kind of pressure, on such a young girl. I had heard about other guys who got married then immediately went off to war and got themselves killed. I cared too much for this girl to put us through that. I knew that I wanted to spend the rest of my life with her, but I had to get this out of my system first. She needed to focus on graduating from school, and not on her boyfriend who was on the other side of the world. We both needed to mature a lot, before we jumped off into a marriage. This would certainly be the ultimate test, of our love for each other. We tried to make my last few weeks at home very special, and we spent as much time together, as was possible.

My family had all finally accepted my decision and were treating me real good. The days flew by, and all of a sudden, it was time for me to leave. The day that I left home was a miserable time for me, and I'm sure for my family and Faye, also. I had to act brave, so somehow I managed to keep from crying. I promised to write often. I told them that I loved them and would be seeing them real soon.

Chapter 2

ROUGH DAYS AHEAD

My military career began with basic training at Fort Polk, Louisiana. This place had been labeled with several names, but I probably don't need to repeat them. I had heard a lot of horror stories about this place and basic training, but it was like nothing that I could have imagined. The days were long and the nights were short. I was intimidated by the size of the other fellows, but I fit in real well, and made a lot of friends. I was very determined and I was going to give them one hundred percent. I had always worked on the farms, so I was in pretty good physical condition. I didn't have any trouble with the training and I actually enjoyed most of it. I was truly amazed with the fact that so many young men had never even held a gun in their hands.

Cultures vary tremendously throughout areas of the United States. I had done very little traveling during my earlier years, and I enjoyed listening to guys tell about their different lifestyles. The nine weeks of basic flew by a lot quicker than I had expected them to. Some of the guys couldn't make it through Basic Training and were rotated out of the Army with a Undesirable Discharge. I sure didn't want something like that on my record for the rest of my life. My family and Faye came to see me when I graduated from basic training, and they all seemed very proud of me. I was sure proud of myself. I must admit that I thought that I looked pretty good in my dress uniform.

My next duty station would be at Fort Gordon, Georgia, where I would enter my advanced infantry training. They had portions of this camp set up, to resemble Vietnam. They had mock villages, VC base camps, booby traps, and even an active landmine field. Some of the advanced soldiers were given the roles as enemy soldiers. This training should prepare us for the obstacles, that would be awaiting us in Vietnam, and hopefully keep us alive. I especially enjoyed this phase of my training, because it taught us how to use all different types of weapons. They even familiarized us with weapons that the enemy would be using. We spent most of our days and nights in the surrounding hills and valleys, and we learned how to survive under all type conditions. I especially enjoyed this part of the training, because I was a country boy, that spent most of his time outside and in the woods.

I excelled in most of the areas of training. At the end of our infantry training, we were given a series of exams. I was told that I had qualified for an opportunity to attend the Army Academy at West Point. They said that it was a privilege and honor to even be considered for this appointment. I don't know how I pulled that one off, because I wasn't exactly a rocket scientist in school. If I chose to go, and completed the program, then I would be commissioned as an officer. Attending this program would require me to sign a six-year contract with the Army, and I would not be allowed to get married during this period. After I considered this option for about ten minutes, I declined the offer and continued to pursue my earlier dreams. Marriage seemed a lot more fun than having bars on my shoulder.

My next big obstacle would be airborne training. This is what the Army has labeled its paratrooper division. This is where one of my childhood dreams would come true. I was going to find out if I really had the guts to jump out of a real airplane. This training would take place at the famous Fort Benning, Georgia. This school would only last for three weeks, though it was supposed to be some of the toughest training that the Army had to offer. I figured that I would be able to stand up under any kind of abuse and treatment for three weeks. Members from all the other branches of the military would also be training with us. There would also be all ranks involved in the activities. I heard that the "Black Hat Sergeants" really liked to pick on the officers.

The airborne training was broken down, into three phases, each lasting one week. The first week was called ground week and it was primarily based around extensive physical training. The purpose of this was to prepare your body for the tremendous impact that happens when you hit the ground. It was unbelievable how hard you land. They told us that it would be like jumping out of a two-story window. A lot of the physical training was running. The "Black Hats" knew how to make it into sheer torture. A lot of the guys dropped out during the ground week. Airborne training is totally voluntary, so you can quit any time during the first two weeks. I never considered this as an option. We were taught how to fall and roll when we made contact with the ground. This would hopefully keep us from breaking any bones. Sometimes it works, and sometimes it doesn't.

The second week was known as tower week. It turned out to be a lot of fun. We continued with the strenuous physical training, but this week involved a lot more. We jumped out of 34-foot towers, went down long cables, and were able to practice our PLF's (parachute landing falls) when we finally hit the ground. Jumping from the towers gave us the feeling of the jerk, which we would encounter when the real parachute would inflate. It also had us strapped in a real jumping harness, so we found out real fast that it was very important to have the straps adjusted properly, especially in the groin area. A few of the guys left the towers with a high-pitched tenor voice. We had several more guys drop out during tower week.

The third and final week was known as jump week or graduation week. The jump week was strictly set aside to make our five parachute jumps that were required to graduate from airborne school. We were told that we could still sissy out, up until the point that we actually boarded the plane for our first jump. They said that once the plane door was closed, that we would have plenty of help going out the door, in case we wanted to back out. Of course, we continued to have physical training, every morning. I had many mixed emotions. I was scared to death, but extremely excited at the same time. We would graduate from jump school when we hit the ground on our fifth jump. The wings would be pinned on our chests, right there on the landing zone.

I had begun to get sick during the middle of tower week, but I wasn't about to tell anyone. After completing my first jump, I was called to the side by one of the "Black Hat" instructors. He said that I looked like death, and he made me go to the dispensary for a checkup. I had a high temperature of 106 degrees, and was told that I had pneumonia. I had to stay in the hospital for about ten days. When I was released from the hospital, they informed me that I would have to start over at the beginning of tower week. At least, they didn't require me to go through ground week again. I completed five more jumps and was awarded my jump wings. That was probably one of the most memorable days of my life. This was a real morale booster for me. I felt that I had accomplished something that very few people would get the chance to do. At that moment, my size didn't seem to matter; I was as big and bad as anyone.

Later that day, we were assembled in formation, to receive our new duty assignments. We had been told that over ninety percent of us would be sent to South Vietnam, for combat. I was excited, because I was looking forward to seeing some real combat. I felt that my training had prepared me for anything. Boy, was I wrong! That was the main reason that I had joined the Army. The sergeant said we would either be assigned to Alaska, Germany, or Vietnam. He said if our name was called out, we were going to Nam, and we should form a group to his right. The ones going to Germany or Alaska should form a group to his left. After about three quarters of the names had been called out, I finally heard mine. My new assignment was to the 8th Army Division, in Bad Kreuznach, Germany. I was overwhelmed with disappointment, but there wasn't anything that I could do about it. I would get to go home for a few days, before I had to ship out. At least, this was good news, because I wanted to show off my paratrooper wings, to Faye and family.

9

CHAPTER 3

FIRST ASSIGNMENT

I was given a ten-day leave at home before I had to report to Fort Dix, New Jersey. This is where we would be processed at and receive all of our gear that we would need while we were in Germany. Faye and I had a wonderful time while I was home on leave, but the time had flown by quickly. She seemed to be real proud of me, and was holding up well. She knew that I was disappointed about not going to Vietnam, but I am sure that she was relieved. It was soon time for me to tell everyone goodbye, again. We were scheduled to spend three to five days in New Jersey, awaiting our flight to Germany. It snowed the entire time that I was there. I'm talking about a major snowstorm. I wasn't used to this because I was a boy from the deep South. I had only seen snow a couple of times in my lifetime. Our days were spent doing all kinds of fun things, like getting a dozen immunization shots, and watching films about the lifestyles of the people who we would be coming in contact with over there. I would not know what my job was until I arrived in the country, and was assigned to a company. The Army enjoys surprising soldiers like that.

The flight to Germany was to be on board a commercial plane, and it should take us about eight hours to reach our destination. This would be the first transcontinental flight that I had ever been on. It was the largest plane that I had ever seen, and it even had movies for us to watch, while we were in-flight. It was fun and eventful, but extremely tiring. I was actually beginning to look forward to seeing parts of Europe. When we finally arrived in Germany, we were divided into groups and trucked to our new assigned units, scattered all over the countryside. I was sent to the 8th Army Division Military Police Company.

I didn't have any military police training, so apparently this was some kind of a mistake. A drill sergeant told me one time that the Army doesn't make mistakes, so this ought to be real interesting. I had heard that one of the qualifications to be a military police was a minimum height of five feet and eleven inches. Apparently, someone had miss measured me, because I was only five feet and two inches tall, at that point of my life. When I checked into my new company, I explained to the first sergeant that a mistake had been made. I told him that I was a trained infantryman and I had volunteered to go to Vietnam. He just laughed and said that I would like it a lot better here, but I was welcome to take my request to the company commander in the morning.

Everyone seemed very nice, and the duty wasn't bad at all. We would pull two weeks of duty on the post, and every third week we would get to work the downtown areas. Most of our patrolling would be done in jeeps, but sedans were used for the downtown duty. We rotated shifts, and were given full privileges, when we were not on duty. This meant that we could stay on the compound, or we could leave and go roaming around. I spent a lot of time walking around in the little town of Bad Kreuznach, and seeing the sights. It was amazing to see how different our culture was from the German way of life. I was brought up in a home where drinking alcohol was not allowed. Over here, it even seemed acceptable for the teenagers to have a drink. Almost everyone drank wine or beer with their meals. Their main sport was soccer, and this was something new for a Mississippi boy, back in the sixties. The little town was located in a valley and was totally surrounded by beautiful mountain ridges. I loved to hike the trails and watch the people below. It was wintertime and there were several inches of snow on the ground. It was beautiful and reminded me of pictures that I had once seen in a magazine.

I had been in Germany a little more than a month, so I decided that it was time for me to have a talk with my commanding officer, about my transfer to a combat unit in Vietnam. I felt that all of my hard training was being wasted here. I requested a meeting with the CO, but was told that I would have to talk with the first sergeant instead. I explained my desires to him and asked for his help in getting me a reassignment. He told me that it was not unusual for a young man to want to see combat. He was a Vietnam veteran himself, so he told me all the reasons, why I didn't want to go over there. He said that I should think about it for a few weeks and, if I still wanted to be reassigned, then he would see what he could do for me.

My best friend and I had a four-day weekend coming up, so we decided to take a trip to Paris, France. We traveled by train and it only took us a few hours to get there. We spent most of our time sightseeing and touring. I was disappointed at how dirty the streets and town were. We had a great time, but it was soon drawing to a close, and we would have to return to work. I took a lot of pictures, so that I would always be able to remember this trip.

I went back to my first sergeant and explained to him that nothing had changed. I still wanted to go to Vietnam and fight for my country. He promised to see what he could do for me. The time was creeping by and I wasn't accomplishing anything. I had been over here about four months now, and the war was raging on without me. My life was simple and easy, but I was bored and miserable.

I had just come off another three day weekend and was scheduled to start downtown patrol that afternoon. I was looking forward to the change of pace and scenery. The shifts always flew by when you were on downtown duty. It had been a quiet night and very little seemed to be going on. It was around 10:30 p.m., and we would be getting off in another thirty minutes. The radio keyed and units were requested to respond to a bar fight at a local tavern where Germans and Americans were known to hang out. It was normally a quiet place of business, but something had sparked some ill feeling among the patrons this fine evening. We arrived with two other military police units and decided to enter the premises together. There were also a couple of German units at the scene. When we entered the building, the place was in turmoil. Glasses and chairs were being hurled through the air and everyone seemed to be fighting someone. I had been in the center of some pretty good bar brawls, but this one was the granddaddy of them all. The Germans and Americans seemed to be about even in number. Even the female patrons were involved in the fist swinging. My eyes were beginning to focus in the semi-dark atmosphere and I could see that several people were down and hurt badly. There was blood and beer all over everything.

I wasn't very far inside the door, when my eyes zeroed in on a big burly German at the bar. He seemed to be zeroed in on me, also. Our eyes met and things went downhill quickly from that point. He pulled out a very large knife, and it was obvious that he was planning on cutting me with it. He started in my direction, and I started hollering, "Halt!" I must have repeated it four or five times, but to no avail. He knew what I was saying, because halt is the German word for stop. I drew out my forty-five caliber pistol and put a large hole in the center of his chest. He hit the floor, only a couple of steps from me. The gunshot seemed to get everyone's attention. After a couple of minutes, the patrons were back under control and the wounded were carted off to the hospital. Some were sent to lockup, but most of them ran out the door and got away.

When we got back to our station, we were all required to write out statements about what had taken place. I was relieved of duty, until a full investigation could be conducted. I was told that I could not leave my barracks, until further notification. I was allowed to go to the mess hall for meals, but that was all. This went on for several days, and finally I was told to report to my commanding officer. My CO said that this could have been a national incident, but one of the German police officers had given a statement that matched mine, and said that I had done everything possible to avoid pulling my weapon. He said that I had shot the man in self-defense. I was placed back on duty, but was removed from the downtown patrol list.

I started visiting my first sergeant on a regular basis, and pestered him about being reassigned to Vietnam. He said that after my little run-in with the German, they would probably be glad to get me over there. I was told to contact our chaplain and see if he could help me out. A chaplain has a lot of pull in the military. I spoke to the chaplain and explained my situation. He echoed the first sergeant's warnings about the dangers, and told me that I was crazy. He asked me if I was a Christian and I assured him that I was. He told me to pray about it for a few days, then come back and we could talk some more. I returned after three days and told him that I still felt the same way. He told me that he would see what he could do. He met with me again that afternoon, and told me that the only way I could leave Germany was to take a 1-year reenlistment extension. If I did that, the Army would have to let me choose my next duty station. I did it and was re-sworn into the Army, again. My three -year hitch in the Army had now turned into four years. I knew that Faye and my family would not be too happy about this decision.

By the end of that week, I had received new orders that would send me to South Vietnam, as an unassigned soldier. The chaplain apologized and said that since I was trained for infantry duty, I would probably bust the front lines wide open. I thanked him for his help, and told him that I was at peace with that situation. I was to be flown out of Germany on the following Monday and would get to spend thirty wonderful days at home prior to my departure to the Republic of South Vietnam. I said goodbye to all my friends and caught the big bird to the States.

CHAPTER 4

IT'S A DOG'S LIFE

There were different purposes for the use of dogs in the Vietnam War. There were those that were trained for tracking duties, and others that were used for sentry or guard duty roles. The dogs and their handlers were put through months of extensive training. The dog's training was dependent upon what job it would be doing once it reached the war-zone. The dog and handler did not necessarily stay together when they reached their assigned destinations. There were usually already dogs in country that needed a handler. Dog handlers, like all other soldiers, sometimes got killed in combat, or their tour of duty may have ended and they went home. Several different breeds of dogs were used, but most of the handlers that I spoke with, preferred the German shepherd. They were taught to obey hand signals, as well as verbal commands. The dogs remained under the watchful eyes of their handler, even when they were off duty. I was told that a dog was a delicacy on a gook's dinner table. I'm not sure if this was true or not, but you sure didn't see many dogs walking around.

The scout dogs were used extensively, with some of the infantry units. They were helpful to locate things like booby traps, ambush sites, tunnels, caches of weapons, food, and other enemy supplies.

The dogs were trained not to bark, because this could alert any enemy soldier who might be in the area. The dogs had different ways of alerting their handler of present danger. Some may get in a point position, like a birddog, and others might stop and refuse to move forward. Usually, the dog would be staring at the danger.

The military police used guard dogs extensively in Vietnam. Most of the larger compounds in Vietnam utilized civilians for all sorts of labor purposes during the day. They were required to vacate the premises before the sun went down. These civilians were checked through a gate, prior to entering the compound. The dogs were used to sniff for weapons, and other types of contraband. They also used them to locate explosives and other possible threats to our soldiers. The dogs were also used at many facilities as backup support on perimeter patrols and guard duty.

There were hundreds of stories about the heroic deeds that dogs accomplished during the Vietnam War. Entire squads have been saved because these dogs have alerted the soldiers prior to their entering a hostile ambush site. They have located snipers when the soldiers were pinned down and could not search for them. Tunnels had been located, and the enemy were killed and their equipment was destroyed. They were able to work in some tighter places and rougher terrain with ease. Their stamina was remarkable and they didn't have to worry about "Dear John" letters.

I did not have a lot of contact with these dogs during my tours in Vietnam. I went on a couple of recon patrols that a scout dog was involved, and we had one flown in by chopper one time to check out a tunnel complex. They were always alert and did an excellent job. You can't help but feel safer when one of them is leading the way, with his nose sniffing the air and ground continuously. They can hear, see, and smell things that the average soldier doesn't know is in the area. I asked one of the handlers how his dog could tell the difference in the scent of a gook and an American soldier. He said that the gook's diet gave him a distinct body odor.

When I arrived in Vietnam, I was introduced to a three-legged dog. I'm not sure what his name used to be, but his present name was Sergeant Tripod. He appeared to be of mixed breeds. One of these must have been a yellow cur dog. He was a friendly fellow and everyone liked him. He had the run of the camp and the chow hall made sure that he had plenty to eat. It wasn't unusual to find him asleep on someone's bunk during the day. He wasn't choosey about whose bunk he got on either.

I was told that he was an ex-recon scout dog, and was a real celebrity around these parts. He had seen several firefights and been in the middle of a couple of major battles. He was accredited with having saved many American lives. He wore a set of dog tags which read Sergeant Tripod in bold letters. He had been wounded in a firefight during one of his many missions. He was shot in the left front leg by an AK-47 assault rifle. He was airlifted off the battlefield, with the wounded soldiers, and taken to a hospital, where a surgical veterinarian was waiting. The wound was so serious that they were unable to save his leg, and it had to be amputated. An officer later came to the barracks, to retrieve the dog and have him put to sleep. He said that the dog no longer served a purpose for the military. The soldiers hid him until the officer finally left. I think one of the recon soldiers threatened to put the officer to sleep if he didn't leave, ha.

This dog was amazing, because he could get around better than most dogs with four legs. During an awards ceremony, he had been presented a Purple Heart and a Bronze Star, for meritorious service in combat. Some of the guys got mad, because it wasn't a Silver Star, instead of a Bronze Star. He had also been given a field promotion to the rank of sergeant. He outranked a lot of us here. They actually had a plaque hanging in the dayroom honoring him. It listed his name, rank, and displayed his medals and ribbons. There was a typed letter below the plaque that explained all the circumstances that took place that memorable day when he gave his leg for his fellow comrades.

I told this little story in a humorous manner, but the truth is that dogs served a vital role in the Vietnam War. Many combat soldiers will vouch for their usefulness and heroic acts. Some of us were dummies, and we volunteered to go to war. These poor little guys were all drafted, and didn't have a choice. Be kind to your dog, because he may be asked to serve his country one day.

Chapter 5

"FIRE IN THE HOLE"

The gook had disappeared into thin air. He was the only survivor of a small skirmish that we had earlier, down in the valley. His other three comrades were not so fortunate. We had all come out of this one, without even a scratch. It seemed impossible for him to have escaped from the area. The terrain was flat and open. There were very few obstacles for him to hide behind. One of us would have surely seen him up ahead. The other alternative was that he must have gone in the ground. I had heard other soldiers tell stories about the complex tunnel systems in this country, but I had never seen one myself.

We decided to form our squad into a horizontal line and sweep the area. We felt sure that we would find him under a rock or bush somewhere. We had an ex-Korean soldier in our squad. None of us could pronounce his real name, so we all called him Sam. Sam had been fighting with the Americans in Vietnam for about twenty-two months, and seemed very pleased with his situation. Sam had moved to the United States after being honorably discharged from the Korean Army. He tried several occupations, but was never happy, so he joined the American Army. He volunteered to go to Vietnam, because he said that he was a trained killing machine. He spoke about five languages fluently. One of these languages was Vietnamese, so we used him as an interpreter. He was also an excellent tracker. He could track a gnat crossing a rock, as long as the gnat kept his feet on the rock all the way across. He was also very good at locating booby traps. I asked him how he was able to see these things, and he said that he just looked for anything unusual or out of the ordinary. If something is not supposed to be there, it was put there for a reason. It could be something as simple as broken limbs or twigs, a dead leaf in the middle of live ones, or a dry area on a dew covered ground. His motto was: "Be alert and stay alive." You can't argue with that.

Despite all of Sam's wonderful qualities, he was only a private first class. He had been busted a couple of times for drinking and getting into fights. These fights always seemed to be with officers, and I might add in his defense that he was never on duty when these fights took place. His rank may have been low, but he had already been awarded a Purple Heart, a Silver Star, and a Bronze Star. He was an excellent soldier and could be depended on when things got heated up. He was well liked and looked up to by his peers.

Sam had tracked this fellow to where we were now, but somehow we had lost him. He said that the guy was wounded, but not seriously. He kept pointing out blood spots in the brush, but no one else could see them. We began to sweep the area cautiously. We were moving slowly and trying not to miss anything. We did not know if he had a weapon, because we had found a SKS rifle, along his trail. The barrel was still hot from the recent battle. This was extremely unusual and we were not sure why it was there. He knew that we were hot on his trail and he was in a hurry to get away from us, but a soldier doesn't turn loose of his weapon until he takes his last breath. I have actually seen dead men with a grip on their weapon that was almost impossible to break loose. I guess that is where the phrase "Death Grip" comes from. We had left two men behind to watch our rear and flanks. After covering quite a large area, our squad leader called for us to re-group. Sam had been running around, like a coon dog on a fresh trail, but had not found any sign. The squad leader was frustrated and said that he had received radio orders not to leave the area until this VC was located. We spread out again and started to retrace our steps. Sam reminded everyone that a trapped animal that was wounded was very dangerous and would do anything necessary to escape.

We were about ready to accept defeat again when Sam let out a yell. He was snooping around the area, where he originally had lost the trail. We all mustered around him to see what he had found. He pointed to the ground and said that's where he went. At first, I didn't see a thing, but all of a sudden, I saw the little door. Sam said that one of us should shoot him, for not finding this sooner. We had several volunteers, but the squad leader wouldn't let us. The door was made out of bamboo strips and had a bush, actually growing from the top of it. It fit the hole beneath, perfectly. We tied a piece of string to the bush. Everyone moved a safe distance back, before the door was snatched open. We all had our weapons aimed and were ready for anything that might come out of the hole. We figured the door was booby-trapped, so we expected an explosion. Nothing happened, but we could hear some Vietnamese jabbering coming from the hole. Sam said the VC was begging us not to kill him. He was told to throw out all his weapons and come out of the hole with his hands lifted. Our squad leader was shouting the orders and Sam was repeating them to the VC. He came out with his hands lifted and had no weapons. Sam asked him if anyone else was in the hole, and the gook said that he was by himself. We did not trust him so the order was given to toss a grenade in the hole. As Corporal Johnson released the grenade, he yelled, "Fire in the hole." After the grenade exploded, we checked the hole out. It was no bigger than the bed of a small truck and apparently it had not been used for a very long time. I'm not sure how this guy knew where it was located. Our squad leader had already radioed for a prisoner pickup and the chopper was on the way. Sam interrogated him while we waited on the chopper and asked him why he did not have a weapon. He said that he had a SKS, but lost it when we were chasing him. He had been shot through the right hand during the battle and could only carry the gun in his left hand. The wound in the hand was where the blood spots came from that Sam was tracking. During the chase, he had fallen down and broke his left wrist. He was unable to tote the weapon with either hand, so that is the reason that we found it along the trail. There were some weird things that happened during my two tours in Vietnam. I can only imagine what must have happened to this young lad after he was carried away. Some questions are easier to live with when we don't know the answers.

CHAPTER 6

TOO TIGHT FOR ME

The Mekong Delta was located in the southern portion of Vietnam. It was intertwined with a network of rivers. Some of the best known of these rivers were the Saigon, Vam Co Dong, and Vam Co Tay. All these rivers varied in size and depth during the year, because of the monsoon season. These rivers were patrolled heavily by PBR crews, known as the "Brown Water Navy." These crews ran up and down the river, both day and night, trying to intercept some of the VC infiltrators entering the country of Vietnam from Cambodia. They also helped to cut down on the VC's usage of the rivers, as a means of movement for their supplies and soldiers. They were an easy target for riverside ambushes and their jobs were extremely dangerous and demanding. The boats were heavily armed but a well-planned ambush site at a bend in the river could cause them a lot of heartache. A couple of direct hits from mortars or RPGs could sometimes put one of these boats out of commission or possibly sent it to the bottom of the river. Quite often, two PBR boats would run together, but kept a distance between them. This gave them additional security, in the event of an ambush. They also played a vital role in picking up wounded or dead grunts who had been involved in a battle upriver. A PBR crew usually consisted of five men. All these guys who I have ever met were highly decorated and distinguished veterans. There are many documented battles that involved the PBR boats in this region of Vietnam.

The Mekong Delta was also the home of a lot of rubber tree plantations. Most of these plantations were owned by the French. Some of these plantations were used as base camps for major groups of enemy troops. The heavy concentration of underbrush allowed them more cover and places to hide. There were heavily used enemy trails, through most of these plantations. The VC seemed to feel secure, as they moved around in the daylight hours. The armored units were sometimes used to recon these areas. One of the most famous of the rubber plantations was "Ho Bo Woods." It was covered with tunnels and entire complexes underground. These tunnels were used by the VC for bivouac facilities, as well as for storage of supplies.

The French military had encountered some bloody battles with the VC in the Mekong Delta and the Americans ran into some of the same types of resistance. The gooks had spent many years preparing this region for battle and it was almost impossible to overpower them and gain control of the area. This was basically a paradise for their style of warfare. Besides the enemy, everything else seemed to be stacked against the Americans and their allies. Other deterrents were; weather, terrain, snakes, insects, rats, dysentery, and leeches. Morale stayed at an all-time low, because of the constant enemy contact and the loss of American lives. Even if we won the battles, there was always another one waiting for us tomorrow. Time crept by and there seemed to be nothing to look forward to. When we got a day off, we spent most of it dreading our next mission. We were scared to form any close friendships, because they might be the next one that you had to help put in a body bag. I was only eighteen years old, but I felt like I had already seen more death and destruction than a person should have to witness in an entire lifetime. The worst part was that I had only been in Vietnam a little over two months and I had another nine months to go. I wasn't sure if I would be able to hold up and take it.

Our next mission was going to be a big one. It was listed under "special operations" and would involve the joint efforts of several units. This would even involve some ARVN soldiers and a small squad of Korean mercenaries. We were going to make a massive "search and destroy" sweep through one of the rubber tree plantations. This particular plantation was known as the Fil Hol Plantation. It was owned by the French and was thought to be the home of several VC regiments. This area had been left alone for a while, so the enemy resistance was sure to be strong. There would be more than a hundred of us ground stompers and we would be supported by a unit of armored APCs. During our briefing, they said that the underbrush would make our mission tough and it could even slow down the APCs. I didn't think that anything could hamper the path of one of these things. They said that the VC could hide almost anywhere and the area was covered with trenches and tunnels. We could also call in help from the air, in the areas that the terrain would allow it.

We would not be able to use a normal horizontal sweep pattern in a lot of the section, due to the heavy underbrush. We would have to break up in squads and travel some of the paths.

And this would certainly add many additional risks. This would make it a lot easier for Charlie to use booby traps and have ambushes waiting on us. Not only do booby traps maim and kill soldiers, but also they alert the enemy of our advancing in their area. Our casualties were sure to be tremendous, but the military's intelligence group felt that it would be well worth the losses. Of course, none of these decision-makers would be going along on this mission. It's a good thing that we were not allowed to put it to a democratic vote.

The Army has a special unit called the "Tunnel Rats." These guys were a special breed of soldier. They were all small in stature but you didn't want to mess with them. They were combat ready and capable of getting the job done. Most of the tunnels in Vietnam had small entries and passageways, because the Vietnamese people were extremely small. When a tunnel was located, the Tunnel Rats would be called in to enter it and check the situation out. They never knew what was waiting for them, below the ground surface. The VC were known to put all sorts of harmful things in these tunnels such as booby traps, deadly poisonous snakes, and punji sticks. If an explosive booby trap was detonated, you not only had to worry about losing body parts but staying alive. Of course, there was always the chance of crawling into a room full of VC who knew you were coming and had a welcoming party prepared for you. The normal working gear of a tunnel rat consisted of a flashlight, small pair of cutting pliers, a K-Bar survival knife, and a forty-five caliber pistol. They usually didn't have room to take anything else with them. Sometimes they would have a rope tied around one of their legs, as they entered the tunnel. I was told that this was so they could be pulled back out in the event of trouble or injury. This had to be a voluntary unit, because everyone that I met was gung ho and ready for the next mission. I sure didn't have the guts to be a part of this group.

We entered the woods, just as the dawn was breaking across the horizon. This was one of those colorful sun risings that should make everyone realize that there is a God out there. I was awestruck by the beauty, and then a chill crept across my body and brought my mind back to the present reality of war. The remainder of this day was sure to bring many bloody encounters and each one would end the lives of both Americans and enemy soldiers. I glanced around me at the other soldiers and wondered if they were scared like me. I was still a child in many ways but the last few months had made some changes in me that I wasn't real thrilled about. The value of a human life did not seem as important anymore. I wanted to discuss my feelings with someone, but I was sure that they would laugh at me. I had to put all these silly thoughts out of my mind and focus on surviving this mission. Our officers wanted a high enemy body count and that was all that mattered right now. I had already been promoted to corporal since I got over here, so I must be doing a pretty good job.

The first gunshots rang out to let us know that the initial enemy contact had been made. It was a short burst of M-16 fire, so I figured that one of the soldiers had crossed paths with one or two unsuspecting gooks. This would alert the others in the area, and the rest of the day would not be so easy. The next sounds that we heard was about a half hour later and they came from an AK 47. An AK-47 assault rifle had a unique sound when fired, and it was easily recognized by a seasoned combat veteran. It was probably a sniper in one of the trees. A short firefight transpired, and then everything went quiet again. We kept hearing an occasional exchange of fire in several different directions, but my group had still not made enemy contact. My feelings were not hurt at all. There was a couple of APCs moving through the brush to our right and they were knocking things down and making a terrible racket. We had found a couple of abandoned bunkers and one grenade booby trap but had not seen any gooks. We had entered an open area, so the sergeant suggested that we stay in the tree line and circle the area. This would cut down on the chance of getting pinned down by an ambush. Just as we successfully made it around the opening, a mortar round exploded in the trees to our left. One of the guys got shrapnel in his leg but it wasn't life threatening. We were not sure where the mortar had come from, so we quickly set up a small perimeter until the medic could check out the wounded man. He was bandaged and we proceeded through the woods. One of our guys spotted a well-concealed bunker, and we figured that the mortar had originated from there. We lobbed a couple of M-79 grenade rounds onto the site, and then several soldiers rushed the position, to check it out. A hand grenade was tossed into the mortar tube opening and it set off all the excess mortar rounds. It caused a considerable explosion. It was hard to tell from the pile of body parts, but I think there were three gooks inside the bunker. The next few hours were pretty much the same. Firefights were going on in every direction and we got into a few scraps ourselves. We found several trenches and a small tunnel that was no longer in use, because parts of it had caved in. We heard on the radio that and APC had ran one track off in a concealed tunnel and could not get out. They would have to bring in the vehicle, called a tank-retriever, to pull it out.

Later that day, we stumbled across the entry of a tunnel, which seemed to be well used. None of our guys would fit into the opening (or at least that was the excuse that we used), so we radioed for the pros. A little while later, a five-man tunnel rat team showed up to take charge of the situation. They looked at the hole, spread out and checked the surrounding area, then got in a huddle to plan their strategy. They could not locate an exit hole, so they were concerned about the complexity of the tunnel facility. They said that the angle of the hole and the extremely small size told them that this might not be the main entrance to the tunnel. They thought that the tunnel complex was very deep and large. We were asked to spread out and check the surrounding area for other signs. We figured that they wanted to find the main entrance and go in that way, but they said that they always preferred entering through a back door. I'm not sure how they determined which one of them would be the lucky one to enter the hole first, but the little guy seemed ready and anxious to get started. They first checked around the hole and down in the entryway for booby traps. The tunnel rat gave the others a thumbs up and dove into the hole, head first, with the aid of his buddies. He had a flashlight in one hand and a forty-five caliber pistol in the other. His knife was in a scabbard across his chest. I got scared just watching him disappear into the hole. I have never been fond of being in a tight place, especially when it is dark. After what seemed like an eternity, but in reality was only a few minutes, the soldier's head popped out of the hole. He was covered in dirt from head to toe. I was wondering how he had managed to turn around in that little hole. He said that he had followed the tunnel for about twelve or so meters, then it opened up into a large room. The tunnel proceeded out the other side and he figured that it would lead to other rooms. He wanted some backup before he checked it any further. Two more tunnel rats prepared their equipment for the entry. The little soldiers did not think that they would encounter any problems because he felt like the tunnel was presently under construction and had not been completed yet. He said the dirt on the floor and walls looked fresh.

The three of them followed each other back into the hole. The two who stayed behind listened intently for instructions from their buddies. All we could do was sit around and wait for their return. Finally, the first head popped out and the three tunnel rats emerged. They all huddled together again, and started discussing their findings. It was as if the rest of us did not exist. Our sergeant finally butted in and asked what was going on. We were told that the complex consisted of two major rooms, but it was obvious that more were to be added later. The plan was for it to be a major underground facility. A chopper dropped in some supplies that the tunnel rats had radioed for. They were going back in to set up a series of demolitions that would cause the tunnel to cave in and be destroyed. The same three went back in and took some of the supplies with them. Every few minutes, one would come back out and get additional supplies. They always went back in the hole, head first. When the tunnel rats completed their job, the explosives were detonated, and when the ground finally stopped shaking, there was nothing left but a giant crater. I guess that the enemy, that had been working on this tunnel had left the area when they found out we were headed in their direction. I was sure proud of that.

As the day came to a close, we reached our designated pickup point and caught the choppers back to the base camp. I never heard the results of the mission, but the officers seemed pleased. Apparently, we had racked up several dozen dead enemy soldiers and one group had captured two enemy prisoners. Our main accomplishment was the destruction of many bivouacs and hiding areas for the VC. Now it would be much easier and safer for the next task force to enter the plantation, and destroy more of the enemy troops. We lost a couple of fallen comrades and several were wounded but it was certainly a lot better than I had expected. I take my hat off to the soldiers that served as "Tunnel Rats." My squad was shipped out a couple of days later and I never had to return to that area of Vietnam, known as the Mekong Delta. I would have to be haunted by some of its memories for the rest of my life. I wonder if the central highlands are going to be any better, ha.

CHAPTER 7

THE SHOW MUST GO ON

During the last part of 1969, my group was pulling short recon missions, deep in the Mekong Delta. We were usually out in the bush, three to four days at a time. We were based out of a little camp in Tra Cu. The main purpose for this base camp was a home for Green Beret "A" teams. There were also Cambodian mercenaries and Special Forces from South Vietnam. There were several rivers in this area, and some of our missions would take us along their banks. One of these rivers was the Vam Co Dong and had been renamed as the "River of Death." We would sometimes cross paths with the riverboats that patrolled these waters. The little camp at Tra Cu was called "Hell on Earth." The "A" team members shared stories with us that would make the hair stand up on the back of your neck. They said that if you counted both KIAs and WIAs that the results would be above 100%of Tra Cu's American forces. Most of these guys had at least one Purple Heart and some of them had several.

The Viet Cong activity in this region was truly unbelievable. We were working with a thirteen man recon squad. Our major mission was to set up ambush sites and stop enemy troops from entering Vietnam from Cambodia, by way of the Ho Chi Minh Trail. We were involved with some type of enemy contact, almost every day and night. We would reposition ourselves regularly, and each time the new site seemed to be hotter than the last. Sometimes, we would be in several different firefights, in the same 24-hour period. We were racking up an impressive number of VC kills, but we had to pay for it dearly. There was hardly a day that went by, that we didn't have to radio for a dust-off chopper to pick up a wounded or fallen squad member. We received replacement soldiers continuously. Some of these guys would be brand new in country. I had only been in Vietnam about three months myself. This was definitely not a good place to get your initial combat training.

Each mission was pretty much the same. The choppers would take us to a designated area, and drop us off. It wasn't unusual for the choppers to receive small arms fire from the ground, while transporting us to the mission site. After we were on the ground, we would recon for a short time, and then set up an ambush perimeter. Each mission was spent in a relatively small area. Sometimes we would move several times during the day, but we never moved very far at a time. Any time we had enemy contact and gunshots were exchanged, we would relocate as soon as the battle was over. Our squad leader said this was to keep the enemy from locating us, because he was sure some of them had heard the battle. We would move our wounded and dead with us. They would be airlifted out; when he thought the area was safe. This type of fighting was totally different than anything I had done before. I was used to humping through the bush all day, and being dog tired with sore feet at night. Our night ambush sites took a lot more preparation. We put out trip flares, claymore mines, and the whole welcoming selection of surprises. We never moved around at night, we settled in and stayed in place. The day ambushes seemed to be more successful. At least, we were usually able to take out a few stragglers that wondered through the area.

Christmas was only a couple of days away, and it was obvious that we were all showing extra signs of depression. This was my second Christmas in the military, but my first one to be on the other side of the world, in a war zone. The VC had promised a cease-fire during Christmas, but we had been warned that it may not happen. My squad was scheduled to enjoy a couple of Christmas holidays at the Tra Cu base camp. We got word that the Bob Hope (USO) Christmas Show would be at Cu Chi this year. Apparently, Cu Chi wasn't very far to the east of our present location. We started making plans to go see the show. This would have to be the highlight of any grunt's Vietnam tour. We tried to bribe every chopper pilot in the area, but were unsuccessful. The only other option was to try and find an available deuce and a half truck. We needed a large enough truck, to hold our entire squad. This idea wasn't going very well, either. We were all depressed and about ready to give up the whole idea. One of the guys got word of a supply convoy, that would be leaving Tra Cu on the very morning of the show, and it would be going straight to Cu Chi. The officer in charge of the convoy agreed to let us go, as additional security guards. We would be divided up among the vehicles, but we didn't mind at all. We would reach our destination, well before show time.

We left out with the convoy around daybreak that morning and should arrive in Cu Chi, with several hours to spare. We were heavily armed and prepared to defend the convoy, but that was the last thing on our minds. We were all happy and joking with each other, because we were on the way to see the Bob Hope Show, and nothing could stop us now.

Everything was going great, until we rounded a sharp curve, which took us near the riverbank. This area had a lot of dense vegetation that the enemy was using to conceal themselves. All of a sudden, our happy little world was turned upside down. They hit us with automatic weapons, RPGs, mortars, and other assorted weapons. The lead vehicle had been taken out, and several other properly placed rounds had managed to bring our convoy to a halt. Vehicles were exploding and men were screaming in pain. The attack seemed to be coming, totally from the river side of the road, so we all started retreating to the other side and took cover. It was obvious that we had many casualties and our situation looked bleak. We were trying to communicate with each other and obtain some type of order, but it was a mass confusion and total chaos. It appeared that all our commo equipment had been destroyed in the initial attack. We had no way to radio for help. We had begun this trip with over twenty vehicles and approximately eighty soldiers. We now hoped that half of these men were still alive, and none of the vehicles were operational. I prayed that a chopper would fly over and see the battle raging below. One of the guys said that they would send help when we didn't arrive in Cu Chi. I had my doubts about that, because everyone was too worried about the Bob Hope Show to miss any of us. So far, only eight of our squad members were accounted for.

The smoke from the exploding vehicles had allowed our surviving guys, to safely find refuge for the moment. We should be able to put up a good fight, and defend ourselves for a short time. I hoped that everyone had a weapon and plenty of ammo. I was in pretty good shape. I had a couple hundred rounds for my M-16 and two frag grenades. We had no idea how large the enemy force was, but if they tried to advance on us, we would let them know that they had a tiger by the tail. We were pinned down, but were holding our own. They must have used all the heavy artillery to knock out the convoy, because all we were receiving was smallarms fire. Neither side seemed brave enough to try any heroic deeds. Our biggest fear was that other VC were in the area, and would be coming soon. We were in a good position to fight off a small frontal assault, but not if we were flanked or attacked from the rear. This occasional exchange of fire went on for several hours. I think we lost one more man during this period and we heard a couple of theirs yell out in return of our gunshots. I hurled one of my grenades into an area where there seemed to be several enemy. I heard a couple of painful responses from this. As the day drug on, the time was a factor against us, because we were in the middle of enemy territory and probably nobody knew that we were in trouble. A couple of our survivors were wounded, but not seriously. I had forgotten all about the Bob Hope Show and was trying to focus on my survival instincts. When I came to Vietnam, I had made a vow to myself that I would not allow myself to be taken alive as a prisoner. We were a long way from that, but the options were running through my mind. At a time like this, a person's mind will begin to wonder. I was thinking about my family, and especially about Faye, that I would probably never get to see again. She was real young and I was sure, that with time, she would be able to get over me and move on with her life.

We began to hear movement from our rear, and it was obvious that more enemy had arrived and were boxing us in. We had to re-adjust our perimeter and every other man faced the rear and prepared for an attack. We knew now that it would only be a short time till we would be overrun. I could hear some of the guys praying aloud and making promises to God that they would never keep. It's amazing how humble a person can become, when he is facing death.

The assault begun and we were being hammered from both sides. We could hear whistles being blown and commands being shouted. The Viet Cong used whistles to give commands to their troops during a battle. We were trying to return fire, but they pretty well had us at their mercy. This went on for about half an hour and we began to hear the rear force advancing closer to our positions. I looked down and made sure that my K-Bar knife was in the scabbard, because I would use it to end my problems, if we got overrun.

Above the battle sounds, I could hear the thump-thump of choppers, as they were getting near. Sure enough, the cavalry was on the way. The Cobra gunships began to release everything they had on the gooks across the road. They totally annihilated them. This was probably the most wonderful thing that I had ever seen, but it was scary too, because it was taking place across the road from where I was lying. The rear enemy force saw what was happening to their little buddies, and retreated in every direction. The Cobras were taking some of them out also, but I am sure that some must have got away. The whole thing was over in minutes. A couple of Chinook medical evacuation helicopters were brought in to remove the American KIAs and WIAs. We were all taken to Cu Chi, but too late for the Bob Hope Show. This was one of the worst days that I spent in Vietnam. We were under attack and pinned down for over eight hours. We had thirty-nine casualties and eighteen wounded Americans. Only eight of my thirteen-man squad walked away from this battle. I never heard the enemy body count.

You might remember earlier in my story that I said I had prayed for a chopper to fly over and see the battle going on. That is exactly what really happened. A reconnaissance chopper was flying over and spotted all the smoke. He came in for a closer look and viewed the ongoing battle. He radioed ahead to Cu Chi and the Cobras were dispatched to our rescue. It was amazing how accurate the Cobras were able to do their jobs, without any communication from us. Even though many men lost their lives that day, God answered my prayer and was in control of everything and looks out for his own, even when they put themselves in bad situations of the entire rescue mission. It's a shame that it took me so many years to realize this.

CHAPTER 8

THE LONGEST THREE MINUTES

The day was just beginning to dawn. There was just enough light, to make out the shapes of a few trees and plants, on the jungle floor. It seems like everything was part of a dream. It had been a miserable and restless night. It was the beginning of the monsoon season, so it had drizzled rain most of the night, and the insects were especially active.

I was a member of an Army Special Forces reconnaissance team, on another search and destroy mission, in the beautiful and tropical Republic of South Vietnam. All of our intelligence reports said that we should be in the middle of an extremely big infiltration of North Vietnamese regular troops. They were more highly trained and better equipped than the enemy troops that we normally ran across. Late yesterday afternoon, we had set up a night ambush site, and had expected to make enemy contact during the night. We were on one hundred percent alert all night, so none of us got any sleep.

We pulled out on patrol at the first sign of daylight. Our squad leader had placed Sergeant Sheppard in the point-man position. This person was in total control of leading the squad on the patrol, and usually was the first one to make contact with the enemy. He had to be the eyes and ears, for the rest of the group. Sgt. Sheppard was chosen for the job, because he was on his third combat tour in Vietnam, and had more experience in the field than any of us. We all felt safe when he was walking in the point position. We felt sure that he would spot the enemy, before they could see us and, he was the also the best at spotting trip wires and other indications that booby traps or mines might be in our pathway. The terrain made it extremely easy, for the enemy to camouflage their little surprises, which could wound or kill any one of us, at any moment. There was no way to be too careful out here.

Our recon team only consisted of thirteen men on this mission. We were armed with M-16s, M-79 grenade launchers, and other assortments of small arms weaponry. I was placed in the number four position and was carrying an M-60 machine gun. It was a little heavier than the other weapons, but I did not mind because it put out a lot more firepower. I had only been in country about five months and I still had a lot to learn from the seasoned veterans. There was no place for overconfidence in the bush.

We started down the trail, and everyone seemed especially edgy this morning. We all knew that the cards were stacked against us, and there were no backup units close by in case we got into any trouble. Sgt. Sheppard started out real slow, and was only covering about ten feet every minute. We would take a couple of steps, then stop and listen, while he surveyed the ground in front of him. It was like he had some kind of sixth sense. It was real foggy and everything seemed ghostly and in slow motion. There was a little light now, and for some reason, I glanced down at my watch to see what time it was. Time makes no difference, when you are out on one of these patrols. You are only thinking about living to see another day.

We had only covered about the length of two football fields when the silence was broken and the whole world was exploding with small arms fire. We had walked into a wellconcealed ambush, and we were receiving gunfire from every side. They had held their fire until they had us totally boxed in. I could hear my fellow squad members screaming from pain and fear. I was too busy firing my machine gun into the brush to know what was going on around me. It seemed like the battle went on forever, but suddenly the shooting stopped as quickly as it had begun. I noticed that I was down on one knee, but didn't remember getting in that position. One of the other squad members ran up beside me and dove down on his belly. He said that he thought that the rest of the squad was dead. We didn't know what to do, because we were not sure if all of the enemy had been killed, or maybe they were getting ready to make another assault on us. We knew that if they came at us again we would not have a chance to fight them off by ourselves. We lay on our bellies, side by side, but facing the opposite direction. This way we could watch all of our flanks, in case the enemy returned. I told the other soldier to start yelling out the names of each squad member, to see if anyone else was still alive. I grabbed our team radio and was going to call in for air support. I glanced at my watch and realized that the entire firefight had only lasted three minutes. I relayed our situation over the radio, and requested some support. We were assured that air support and ground troops would be dispatched to our location, within a few minutes. There had been no response from any of our buddies, so we felt sure that they were all dead. We were totally on our own out here, until the help arrived.

When I laid the radio back down, I must have brushed my side, because I noticed that my arm was covered in blood. I immediately felt a burning, throbbing pain in my left side. I had been shot in the side, below the belt line, and didn't even know when it had happened. During the firefight, my adrenaline was pumping so hard, that I didn't even feel the bullet enter my body and exit in the back. I told my buddy that I had been shot and he just looked at me with amazement.

Again, it seemed like an eternity, but I am sure that it was only a very few minutes before we heard the familiar sound of the choppers coming in fast and low. I popped a green smoke grenade, so they could pinpoint our exact location. The gunships radioed and confirmed the color of our smoke, then they continued to circle our location, until friendly ground troops made it to us. The support soldiers immediately began to sweep the area and search for remaining enemy, and get an accurate body count for the brass. The body count was the most important part of any battle, to the officers. If the enemy lost more soldiers than we did, then the battle was a success. It's hard to stare into the face of a fallen comrade, and see something good or successful about it.

During the three-minute battle, eleven American soldiers and eighteen enemy soldiers had lost their lives. Twenty-nine lives had ended just that quickly. We will never know if we had killed all the enemy soldiers, or if they withdrew prematurely and our two lives were spared. This was definitely another time that God was looking out for me. They loaded me into one of the medevac choppers and took me to the nearest field hospital. I was told that I had been shot by an AK-47 assault rifle and the bullet had passed all the way through my body, without making contact with any vital organs. The doctor basically just cleaned my wounds and patched up both holes. The doc said that I could pick up my weapon and gear, and return to my unit for my next combat assignment. I was assigned to a new squad and was back in the field on patrol, within a couple of days. I realized how blessed I had been and just how close I had come to being killed. I think that it probably made me a lot better soldier and I knew that there were no promises of tomorrow in this crazy place. This ended and began another era in my nineteen-month tour of duty in Vietnam.

CHAPTER 9
TOWER #23

Most of the permanent military reservations in Vietnam were surrounded by guard towers. These towers resembled the fire observation towers found in many regions of the United States. They were constructed of heavy timber, and sit on stilts. The room portion was usually about eight feet by eight feet square. The walls were about four feet high and covered by several rows of sand bags. There was an open space between the top of the wall and the ceiling. This opening was for observation purposes and to shoot out of. The ceiling was also covered by sand bags. The tower could usually stand up under mortar attacks and a barrage of small rockets. The height of these towers would vary, depending on the terrain that surrounded the compound perimeter. The entire perimeter was stretched with strands of barbed wire and interlaced with concertina wire. The concertina wire was covered with razor-sharp barbs. The towers were inside this wire perimeter.

Upon entering one of these compounds, you got the feeling of being inside a maximum security prison. The number of towers or their spacing depended on the size of the compound and what was being guarded. The facilities varied from small firebases, to airstrips and ammunition storage sites. The compounds might be the home of a few dozen soldiers, or possibly thousands.

Tower guard duty was usually assigned to infantry soldiers who were new in the country of Vietnam. This was an easy way to introduce them to the miseries that were in store for them during their twelve-month hitch in country. No matter how much training a person has gone through, his mind and body must make some serious adjustments, when entering a war zone for the first time. The two most important lessons that a soldier must learn are how to be scared and how to depend on a buddy that is also scared. Tower guard duty allowed your body to get used to the climate, at least for the present season. I saw the temperature reach as high as 128 degrees Fahrenheit and we thought that we were going to melt. During the monsoon season, the temperature would drop down in the 60s, and we would almost freeze to death. We would literally have to wear our field jackets to keep warm. Your emotions are so confused, that you have trouble sleeping, and even your appetite is messed up.

The life of a tower guard is usually routine and very boring. When he is not on duty, he resides in a barracks, with all the other tower guards. They usually work twelve-hour shifts and there are two guards in each tower. Only one man is required to be on watch, but they both must remain in the tower during the shift. They can divide their watch time, as they see fit. They are only allowed to come down out of the towers, for rest room breaks and to retrieve their meals, which are delivered to the bottom of each tower. A truck drives around the perimeter at meal times and drops off the food to each location. The sergeant of the guard also makes periodic rounds, to make sure the guards are alert and doing their jobs. The guard that is not on watch can use his spare time any way he wants. He can sleep, play cards, write letters, clean his weapon, etc.

Each guardhouse is furnished with an M-60 machine gun and an M-79 grenade launcher. Both of these weapons are to be cleaned during each twelve-hour shift. Each guard also brings his M-16 rifle with him. Most of the daytime shifts are spent watching the local farmers working in their fields with their water buffalo. An occasional child would come up to the perimeter fence and try to entice the guard to buy some of their goods. Their best seller was home-grown marijuana cigarettes. The guards were not supposed to communicate with them, but sometimes they would. The nighttime duty was much tenser. Some of the towers had giant spotlights in them, so the guards stayed busy scanning the terrain for movement. The shadows were eerie and would make your imagination run wild. If we thought that we saw something, we would pop a parachute flare and it would give us a different view of the area. We had radios in each tower and we could report any suspicious activity. We were not supposed to shoot at anything, unless we were fired at first, or we had been given permission from the sergeant of the guard by radio. Periodically, we were given permission to test-fire our weapons. Sometimes, a sniper would take a few shots at us. These seemed more for harassment than for accuracy. However, occasionally they would luck up and hit a guard. These attacks were consistent enough that it kept us alert and on our toes.

The military compound in An Khe was the home of one of the largest ammunition storage depots in South Vietnam. It housed everything from large bombs to small arms ammo. The perimeter was impressive, with its multiple rows of wire and the towers were located really close to each other. My squad had been temporarily brought out of the field and would have to pull some guard duty for a couple of weeks. We were told that their tower guards saw action regularly. We were used to combat so we were excited about the possibility. I wasn't scheduled to go on guard until the next afternoon, so I would use my time cleaning my gear and catching up on some letter writing. It would also be nice to sit down, to a couple of hot meals. Of course, there was also a hot shower and sleep in a bed to look forward to. The time flew by and before I knew it, I was grabbing my gear and loading onto the deuce and a half that would deliver the guards to our assigned towers.

I was assigned to tower #23 with Johnathan Sands. We had been out on several recon patrols together and knew each other pretty good. We decided to pull three-hour shifts and rotate. I volunteered to take the first watch, because he had done some heavy drinking the night before, and could use a couple more hours of sleep. He settled down and I started checking our weapons. These towers were even equipped with detonators for claymore mines. The mines were placed in several locations amid the wire fencing of the perimeter. Our shift had begun at 6 p.m., so there was still a little daylight left. There were a couple of water buffalo grazing, about 100 meters in front of our tower. The time passed by rather quickly and before I knew it, I was waking up Johnathan for his turn on watch. The short sleep had done him a world of good. I wasn't really tired but I decided to try and get some rest, anyway. I figured my next shift would be boring and tiring. I must have been more exhausted than I thought, because I slept like a log. When he touched me, I sprang to life. It was midnight and time for my next watch. Before lying down, he assured me that all was quiet and secure. The biggest problem that a tower guard has, is staying awake. It can really get boring when there is nothing going on out there. Falling asleep was not a problem for Johnathan or myself, because we had been through an ambush out in the field, and knew exactly what could happen if you are not ready. The time passed by slowly. I continually scanned the area with our spotlight. I popped one parachute flare, because I thought there was some movement. It turned out to be a couple of rabbits in love. They sure would have tasted good in a stew. Around 2:30 a.m., the guard in tower #24 had woken his buddy up and they were reporting movement out front. I didn't bother to wake Johnathan up, because they were new guys and I figured that they were seeing ghosts. The sergeant of the guard would be coming out to check on the situation. All of a sudden, I heard a shot ring out and the radio screamed that one of the guards in tower #24 had been hit in the neck. The other poor guy was flipping out. All the towers in this area went to a red alert. This meant that all personnel would be awake and ready for battle. I awoke Johnathan, but told him that I thought it was probably a single sniper. We were all scanning our areas with our spotlights and it looked like a scene out of Hollywood.

Just as things seemed to settle down, a barrage of mortars began to come from the tree line, and one exploded on the center of our roof. The sand bags took the blast well, so all we got was a lot of loose sand. We began to see muzzle flashes from small arms fire, and it appeared that we were in for a full-fledged battle. According to the radios, at least eight towers were receiving heavy fire. We were returning fire but still could not make out many targets. Trucks were arriving and re-enforcements were being placed on the ground to stabilize our perimeter. Now we could see a lot of VC troops, advancing in our direction, slowly. Our machine guns were hammering out rounds to stop this advance. We were definitely slowing them down but some were still coming. Another barrage of mortars was coming in and this was especially detrimental to our troops on the ground. They had very little cover to hide behind. Our spotlight had been shot out and this made us more visible against the skyline. The radio was yelling orders but no one was paying any attention to them. The situation was growing more serious by the moment. The mortars continued and I felt sure that we had many injuries and casualties. They were still too far out for our short-range grenade launchers to be effective, so we kept peppering away with our M-60 machine gun and our M-16s. We would not detonate our claymore mines until they were entering the fence lines. Some of us were popping parachute flares every few minutes to try and give us visible targets. It is hard to shoot at a muzzle flash when it is steadily moving around. The battle continued on, but we seemed to be making some headway. Their numbers were getting smaller, but they continued to advance with the ones left. You could hear the screams of wounded men. I am sure the sounds were coming from both Viet Cong and American soldiers. The stragglers were beginning to enter our first layer of protective wire. We all let loose with everything, even the claymore mines. This finished off the few who were left. The battle was over and the world returned to being deafly quiet. Everyone stayed alert the remainder of the night.

When the sun came up the next morning, the reality of the battle was evident. The scene in front of us was sickening. There were dead enemy soldiers everywhere. A short-range recon patrol was immediately sent out to search the area. They reported 81 dead VC and they brought in three seriously wounded prisoners. The American losses were bad also. We had 4 dead and 31 wounded. Two enemy soldiers had actually broken through our perimeter, and were killed by our ground force. One of these was killed while climbing up the ladder of tower #23. God is good all the time.

47

CHAPTER 10

PINNED-DOWN

The monsoon season was in full swing. It seemed like the entire world was under water. The rivers and streams were swelled out of their banks and all the low-lying open areas looked like large lakes. It was amazing how quickly the water had risen. Most of the wildlife had headed for higher ground and the snakes were everywhere. The snakes seemed very irritable about their present living conditions, so we had to be extra careful, when we encountered one of them. Ants had clustered in large clumps in the taller bushes and on tree limbs.

We had left out on a reconnaissance patrol, a couple of days ago. It was raining when we left the base camp, but not very hard. We had not been in the bush for more than four hours when the bottom fell out. It had been raining hard continuously for the last thirty-six hours, and there wasn't a hint of it easing up. Let me explain a little about the kind of rain that was coming down. It was coming down so hard, that it looked like a large sheet of water falling, instead of individual raindrops. Sometimes, a single drop would hit us and it would actually hurt, because of the size of the drop. We had radioed headquarters yesterday and requested some type of relief. They informed us that all types of aircraft had been grounded for an indefinite period of time and we would have to ride it out. They promised to send some choppers to pick us up as soon as the weather would permit. Some kind of a tropical storm had made a weird turn and was trying to come on shore in our direction. We had managed to get caught in its fury. We still had good radio contact with the guys back at headquarters, so that helped our feelings a little bit. When we had checked in a few minutes earlier, they told us to try and find some shelter, because tornadoes were expected in the area. There wasn't a lot that we could seek refuge under in this particular region. We had spent the first night huddled up to our knees in water on a dike between two submerged rice paddies. The second night, we had been fortunate enough to find a little hill and settle down under some small trees, at the top of it. It was nearing nighttime again, so we would have to find some sort of shelter. Our grid map showed that a nice size hill should be located a short distance to our north. Between the heavy rain and the fog bank, there was no way for us to see the hill in the distance. We would have to use our compass and try to locate it. The wind had picked up and the going was tough. The intelligence reports had assured us of heavy enemy presence in this region, but we felt confident that they would not be moving around in this kind of weather. Charlie didn't mind working at night or in the rain, but this was a little too serious even for them. I just hoped that we didn't stumble into an area where they had taken refuge. We kept in a tight patrol, because it was hard to see the person in front of us.

As we proceeded northward, the trees started getting taller and larger. This was giving us a little relief from the heavy rains, but it also presented some new dangers. The high winds were making the treetops dance around like ballerinas. I expected one of them to break off and fall down on us at any moment. Our pathway began to incline and it was obvious that we were going up the side of a very steep hill. The ground was slippery from the rain and we were having to choose each foothold carefully. As we continued climbing, the hillside was getting steeper and steeper. The rain and fog still did not allow our visibility to be any greater. We had no idea what lay in our pathway ahead, or even how far it was to the top of the hill. Our squad leader halted the patrol and said that we should use the remainder of the daylight to prepare a shelter for the night. He instructed us to dig a trench that would be running vertically up the slope of the mountain. He wanted it to be deep enough for us to be able to sit upright and still have a little clearance above our heads. The width of the trench was large enough for two soldiers to pass each other. The sarge said that he would explain his requests to us later and we would all understand. He wanted the trench dug, in such a way, that if the hole started filling up with water, that most of it would run out the lower end. We would start digging at the high point and work our way to the bottom.

The digging wasn't too bad, because the soil was well saturated with water. Roots from the trees were our biggest obstacles. The hole was filling up with water as quickly as we were digging it, but the slope of the trench was allowing the water to run out the lower end. I wasn't sure if we were accomplishing anything, but I was only following orders. The sarge had a couple of guys cutting limbs off trees and stripping the excess branches from them. He had other soldiers gathering up large rocks. When the trench was finally completed, the squad leader started collecting all of our poncho liners and anything else that could be utilized as roof cover. He started covering the trench at the high end first. He used the tree limbs to lie across the trench on top of the poncho liners, and then he double secured everything by placing heavy rocks around the outer edges of the liners. The tree limbs would keep the liners in place, and also give us some protection, in case a tree blew down and fell across us.

We filled a few sand bags and built a barrier around the top end, to keep water from flowing under the poncho liner and into the trench. We continued this system and worked our way downhill. The top portion of the trench was emptying itself of water. We left a few shooting ports down each side of the trench, in case we had any visitors. The lower end of the trench was also left open, but was well camouflaged with tree branches. We would have enough poncho liners left, to cover a good portion of the floor. Almost all of the water had ran out and I was totally amazed. Sarge said that we were almost finished. We looked at each other, and I think that murder must have been running through most of our minds. He told us to go inside the trench and scrape about two inches of dirt off the walls and remove about four inches from the floor. This would remove all the wet dirt from inside there. It was unbelievable how dry it was when we finally finished. It was well after dark and we were totally exhausted when we finally covered the lower end of the hole. We picked us out a spot and settled down.

We all demanded that the squad leader give us an explanation for this gigantic trench. We could have spent the night in twoman foxholes. Of course, the holes would have filled up with water and we would have been cold and miserable all night. The sarge said that he had been communicating by radio all day and it looked like we would be stuck out here for two or three days. The worst of the weather had not arrived yet, and we should expect it to get more serious. Believe it or not, some officer had given him the details for this shelter. He must have read about it in a book somewhere. The only reason that we would ever go outside the trench would be for the call of the wild. There wasn't room for everyone to lie down at the same time, so we would sleep in shifts, while the others watched through the port holes. We didn't expect any visitors, but you could never be too safe out here. The squad leader radioed headquarters every few hours and the weather didn't seem to be letting up. We ate cold C-rations, because a fire would smoke us out of here. We also didn't need any light sources after dark, because they might be spotted through the port holes or the end opening. We all got some much needed sleep that night, even though our clothes were soaked.

The next morning presented more of the same. The rain may have let up a little but the winds were more ferocious. We had heard a couple of treetops break off and fall during the night. We spent our time cleaning weapons, writing letters by flashlight, and exchanging war stories. Most of the stories were blown way out of proportion, but it at least helped to pass the time. We had a snake enter the trench opening and one of our black soldiers, almost tore the place apart. The sarge threatened to shoot him, if he didn't settle down. The soldier said that he had rather get shot than be bitten by a snake. I don't know what kind of snake it was, but one of the fellows chopped it to pieces, with his entrenching tool. He threw it out the entrance and we all had a good laugh. The black soldier wouldn't talk to any of us, for the rest of the day. He was fairly new in country and hadn't encountered any real snakes yet.

Around mid afternoon, the radio informed us that tornadoes had been sighted in this province. I wondered who was out in this weather looking for tornadoes. We assured them that we were cozy and safe. Our bodies were beginning to ache from the tight and cramped living conditions, but it could be a whole lot worse. One guy went outside to take a leak and when he came back in, he swore that he had watched a tornado pass over his head. I was asleep when all of this took place.

The daylight had almost expired for another day, so we would definitely be staying here throughout the night. I had been in situations where the enemy would have us pinned down and we couldn't move, but this was the first time that I had heard of a patrol being halted for two days, because of the weather. The night dragged by, because we were getting restless. A person can only sleep for so many hours. The sarge received a call on the radio, about 04:00 hours. They seemed to think that we might get a break in the weather after daylight. The winds had almost died down and the rain had slowed to a steady pour. If the rain would slacken a little more, they would try a chopper pickup for us tomorrow. We were told to stay in radio contact for further instructions. I crossed my fingers and went back to sleep. The next morning looked very promising. It was still raining, but only slightly and the fog had almost disappeared.

The radio rang and we were instructed to come back down the hill and patrol eastward, for about two klicks. There was an open area there that the choppers would be able to land and pick us up. We had two hours, to get to the pickup point. We grabbed our poncho liners and equipment, and hit the trail. Normally, we would have used some C-4 or grenades to destroy the trench, but we couldn't take the chance of pinpointing our location to the VC, that were sure to be in the area. We would mark the coordinances and let some aircraft drop some destruction on the area. We arrived at the pickup point, about a half-hour early and formed a line perimeter in the wood line. The choppers arrived and we were airborne in a short time.

Our pilot said that he had spotted a large force of VC, just to the east and headed in our direction. He said that they would have been on top of our position in less than thirty minutes. I was sure looking forward to dry clothes and a hot meal.

CHAPTER 11

CHOPPER-FLOPPER

The next three days would involve an easy mission. I would be going out into the bush with a four-man team. Our job would be to observe and gain information about any enemy activities surrounding our (AO) area of operations. We were told not to engage the enemy unless it became a life-threatening situation. We were all hardened vets and had seen a lot of combat, so it might be difficult to let a Viet Cong soldier just stroll by our positions. So be it, that was our orders for this mission. Our vantage point would be about halfway up the side of a small mountain. We were told that concealment would not be a problem. This portion of the Central Highlands were dotted with lots of hills and covered by small trees and dense underbrush.

We were dropped off a couple clicks from our destination point just after the sun had gone down. This would allow us the opportunity of easing into our bivouac site unobserved. We would have to limit our movements, and have minimal quiet conversation during the next few days. Voices travel easily between hills, especially at night. Along with our normal gear and supplies, we had a couple of cameras and a pair of binoculars. We had notebooks and pencils, to record our findings and support the pictures. Oh yeah, we also brought along a starlight scope. This would help out with the night observations. The starlight scope would intensify an object in the darkness by utilizing light beams reflected from the moon and stars. It is not very effective on a cloudy and moonless night.

The brush and other obstacles on the valley floor were mostly small, so we had very few problems moving toward our destination. We started to cross a very large rice paddy, but decided that it might be a bad idea. The moon was big and bright tonight, and we could easily be seen crossing the open area. It would be worth the extra time and effort to stay in the wood line and go around. As we neared the base of our hill, we decided to sit a few moments and listen to the night sounds in the area and observe the hillside above us for any voices or movements. After about ten minutes, all seemed clear so we proceeded up the side of the mountain. Loose rocks were everywhere, so we had to pick our footing carefully, for safety's sake as well as noise elimination. We found an area, that we thought would be adequate for the night, so we set up shop. We would have two different observation areas, with two men in each one. This would allow one of us to rest, while the other stayed awake. The two areas needed to be fairly close, in the event that something went wrong. We only had one starlight scope and a single pair of binoculars, so we would have to share them with each team. It was well into the night before we settled down, so we didn't expect to see much the first night. We would need to view the surrounding terrain during the daytime, to be able to have a general knowledge of the areas that would be most likely to have any enemy activity. We had our normal defensive devices set up around our positions, but we felt pretty secure.

When daylight came, it promised to be a hot, humid, but clear day. There was a slight breeze blowing around the hillside this morning, so that would help a little bit. Two Air Force fighter jets zoomed low over our positions, headed to some battlefield in the distance. They had probably come from the air strip at Pleiku. We ate a cold C-ration breakfast and exchanged some whispered conversation. The underbrush around us, and the large rocks gave us a good area to move around and still be hidden, so we decided to stay in these positions for now. No one should be able to spot us, unless they were further up on this mountain or saw us through binoculars from one of the other hillsides. Very few gooks had access to binoculars, so we weren't too concerned about that possibility.

There were several different mountain peaks in this vicinity and the valleys were spotted with wooded regions and rice paddies. You could see an occasional thatched hooch, near some of the larger fields. The entire region was intertwined with paths and trails. It was believed that some of these trails were used regularly for VC troops and supply movements. Right now, everything seemed awfully quiet and peaceful down there. We could see a couple farmers working in their fields and a family bathing in a stream. There was a little cloud of smoke coming from one of the other hillsides, but it was surrounded by trees and we could not make out its origin. We suspected a breakfast fire for a small enemy unit. We would keep an eye on it and see if anyone emerged into one of the clearings. We only took a few pictures throughout that entire day. Those were of anyone carrying a weapon or that looked suspicious to us. The night also passed by quietly, except for one particular path down in the valley. Lights kept moving down this path, headed toward the north. Sometimes there would be several lights in a group. The sky had become very overcast and the starlight scope was limited in its usefulness. We guessed that they were enemy troops moving to some build-up area. The groups of lights may have been an enemy supply train.

The next day started out about the same. The farmers were working in their fields and people would occasionally come to the stream to collect water or for bathing purposes. After lunch we observed an enemy recon unit, patrolling down the banks of the stream. There were about a dozen soldiers in the group. Two young ladies were taking a bath around a bend in the stream and when the recon team reached this point, they stopped to enjoy the view. There seemed to be a conversation going on between the girls and the soldiers, but the girls didn't seem to care if they watched them bathe. We had a fairly good view of all of them, through our binoculars. The girls finally came out of the water and proceeded to get dressed in front of the soldiers. By this time, we were fighting over the binoculars. The girls disappeared into the trees and the soldiers started back up the stream. We recorded all of this with photos and notes. One of our guys requested a copy of some of the pictures, ha. As is normal with the Viet Cong, most of their movements took place under the concealment of darkness. The valley floor became very active that night. The skies had cleared up and our old faithful starlight scope was revealing the enemy activity. We recorded more than one hundred personnel moving down the paths below. We even saw an elephant pulling a very large wagon of supplies, down one of the larger trails. The wagon was covered by a tarp and we were not able to see what was under it. It was being led and followed by several NVA soldiers, guarding its contents. We were probably too far away but it was hard to resist, not shooting at them. We had been reporting in with headquarters every few hours by radio. They were excited by our sightings and said that it supported their intelligence reports. We had learned over the previous months that most intelligence reports were not real reliable.

The next morning was extremely hot. There was no breeze and the sun was beating down on us unmercifully. We just wanted the day to pass by as quickly as possible. Maybe the girls would come down to the stream and take another bath. At least that would keep our minds occupied for a few minutes. We were watching a C-7 cargo plane coming out of the south in our direction. It seemed to be flying a lot lower than they normally did. Just prior to reaching our position, some type of rocket came out of the valley treetops and made contact with the small plane. The midsection caught on fire and it was obvious that it was going to crash. We held our breath and waited for the impact. He fought it as best he could, but finally they hit the ground at the base of the hill that was to our front. We radioed in the crash, but headquarters had already received a May Day call from the plane. We were the only friendly ground forces in the area, so we were ordered to abort our mission and head in that direction. They told us to get there as quickly as possible, but use caution because any enemy who saw the crippled plane would be trying to locate the crash site. We estimated that it would take us about an hour and a half to reach the scene. There would be birds in the air shortly to monitor the situation and give necessary air support, but the initial ground contact would have to be made by us. The plane had not exploded on impact so we hoped that the pilots survived the crash and could hang on until we got there.

We hurried down the hillside as quickly as the loose rocks and the bushy terrain would allow. We realized that we might run into a lot of enemy resistance in route, but our adrenaline was pumping and our main concern right now was covering the ground as quickly as possible. We hoped that none of the enemy had seen the exact location of the crash site and would have to waste a lot of time trying to locate it. There was some smoke rising from the crash site but it would be hard to see from most parts of the valley floor. We had plotted a compass course and should be able to go straight to it. As we leveled out on the valley floor, a Cobra gunship few by headed toward the crash site. We had probably covered half the distance and were making great time. We had not encountered any resistance but we were facing two large rice paddies with a large dike dividing them. We had to make a quick decision on whether we would chance crossing the open area, or waste some valuable time going around through the trees. The vote was unanimous and we took off running across the dike. We stayed separated so we would not be as large of a target. We were making a lot of noise and this concerned me, as much as the open space. The dike was probably about 150 yards long, but it looked like a mile across there. A sniper opened fire on us, just before we reached the other side. The bullets were kicking up mud and water around us, but somehow we managed to get safely through them. I remember looking upward and saying "Thank you, God." We didn't have time to deal with the sniper right now, so we proceeded in the direction of the downed plane. Fatigue was wearing heavy on us, but it didn't slow us down. The sniper's gunshots would alert the local VC of our presence. This was not something that a four-man rifle team needed. So far, we had not fired a shot and I hoped that it would stay that way.

We had to be getting very near the crash site. We could see the other hill rising in front of us, so the plane had to be real close. We smelled the aviation fluids before we actually saw the plane. There it was through the trees, and things did not look promising for the crewmembers. The plane had nose-dived into a very large boulder and the front section was demolished. The midsection was still smoldering but there didn't seem to be any reason to fear an explosion. The two crewmembers had been killed on impact. They were broken up and cut up real bad. The Cobra chopper started spraying an area a short distance to our east, with machine gunfire. The radio ordered us to remove the dead crewmen and carry them to an open area, about 200 yards to our west. This was the nearest place for us to be extracted by the helicopters. We would take turns, using the fireman's carry, to transport the bodies. Luckily, neither one of them was extremely large. The Cobra was bouncing around between two areas now and engaging enemy forces on the ground. This meant that the VC were converging on the crash site.

We headed for our pickup point. Upon arriving at the clearing, we laid the bodies down and took up our defensive battle positions, while we waited for our rides. The radio told us that the choppers were about two minutes out, but we could already hear them in the distance. There were two hueys and the clearing was only big enough to accommodate one at a time. The first one set down and we threw the dead pilots aboard and two of our team members followed them. As soon as it left the ground, the other one was coming in fast. As me and my buddy were diving into the chopper door, we could hear the other helicopter taking gunfire from the ground. The gooks were right on top of us, and they started assaulting our bird also. Before the pilot could gain any altitude, a bullet came through the floor and hit the door gunner in the leg. He was losing a lot of blood but he kept hammering the ground with his machine gun. We could hear the bullets hitting the chopper. We had gained a little altitude now but the pilot yelled over his shoulder that they had hit some kind of line and we were losing oil pressure fast. He radioed our position and called for a May Day. We looked at each other and started looking for something to hold on to. The pilot was fighting the controls, but it was obvious that we would not be in the air for much longer. The chopper was flopping around like a wounded chicken. I thought that a grunt should not get killed in a helicopter crash. The chopper pilot yelled for everyone to hang on because we were going in hard. He managed to keep it in the air until we were over a rice paddy. The ground came up fast and we hit hard. The chopper was tilted to the left side and my buddy and I were thrown through the doorway, into the mud. Everything went quiet for a moment.

All of a sudden my buddy said, "Get off of me."

(

"What is your problem?" I laughed and realized that both of us had survived the crash. He was covered from head to toe with mud, but had no visible wounds. I only had a couple of cuts on my left arm. There were five of us in the chopper and we were all alive. We helped the wounded door gunner out and went back to check on the others. The crew chief was in the process of crawling out. He had a nasty cut on his forehead and his nose seemed to be broken. The pilot would survive, but he was in a lot of pain as we dragged him out. He yelled and used some really foul language as he told us what he thought of us. He said that next time he would leave us for the gooks to take care of. I think that his left collarbone, arm, and leg were broken. He also had several deep lacerations on his body. We told him what a great job he had done, but he wasn't very interested in our remarks, at that moment. The Cobra was circling low over our heads. Apparently, he broke off the engagement with the enemy, when he heard our May Day call on the radio. The radio in our chopper was still operational, so we were in communication with everyone. The Cobra pilot assured us that the surrounding area was clear for the moment and a medevac was due at our location in twelve minutes. We had located our weapons and all we could do was wait and listen to the poor pilot moan and groan. The other chopper had made it back to the base camp safely, with the two dead pilots and our other team members. We were rescued shortly and taken home.

CHAPTER 12

I HOPE HE'S EATEN ALREADY

Our squad had been brought in for a few days of in country R & R (rest and recuperation). We were based at Da Nang and were given passes, so that we could go into town and enjoy the local hospitality. We were only allowed to leave the post during daylight hours, because of the constant VC activity in the area. However, some of the MPs could be bribed and they would let us slip out at night. They explained to us that if we got into any trouble that we would be on our own. We figured that we would be able to shoot our way out of there, if things got too rough. When we made trips into town, we always carried our weapons and stayed in groups of four or more. This would allow us to watch each other's backs and be fairly safe. We didn't need a designated driver, but one of us would usually try to stay sober enough to get everyone back to the post.

After three or four wonderful days and nights in Da Nang, our squad leader pulled our passes and told us to be prepared to move out on a short notice. We started re-checking our gear, and got some much needed rest. Late that evening, we were called together for a mission briefing. It seemed that we would be going into the famous A Shau Valley, to pull a reconnaissance mission and set up some ambush sites. We would load onto the helicopters at dawn the next morning.

As we loaded the choppers the next morning, there was a fine mist of rain in the air. We headed due west to our intended destination. We carried thirty-seven recon members on this mission and that was very unusual. We normally averaged thirteen to twenty-one soldiers in our recon teams. The chopper ride would not take but a few minutes, so the new guys would not have much time to get scared. There would be plenty of opportunities for that, once we were on the ground. The pilots put us out in a previously cleared LZ (landing zone) and we all grouped together for further instructions. We were divided into two totally separate recon squads. The teams were labeled as Zebra and Hawkeye teams. These code names would be used for all future radio communications, between the two teams. The mission leader would be with the Zebra team and I was also assigned to it. We would be taking the lead and Hawkeye would follow us, after a twenty-minute interval. The two teams would be in constant contact, by radio communication. This type of patrolling is known as "closing the back door." The Zebra team would be opening the front door and the Hawkeye team would be closing the back door of the operation. This should keep us from being boxed in by an ambush. We would be moving through some very dense rain forest. The visibility was dim and a heavy fog bank added to our problems. The constant rain mist soaked through our clothes and made us miserable. The fog made all our movements look ghostly and in slow motion. I had heard several bizarre stories about the A Shau Valley, and I was beginning to have flashbacks about some of them.

One poor kid was on his first combat mission and he was scared to death. His name was PFC Chris Hargrove. He was a city boy who came from a wealthy family. I think that he was from somewhere in the state of Connecticut. When he graduated from high school, he decided to play around for a couple of years before starting college. Uncle Sam thought that it would be appropriate to give him a job in the Army, so he was drafted into the infantry. He was a very bitter young man and griped about everything. I must admit, there was a lot for him to gripe about right now. He kept telling everybody that he was only nineteen years old and he should not be over here. Heck, I had just turned twenty a few days ago, and I had already volunteered for my second tour in Vietnam. It was quite obvious that this area was used regularly by the VC. The paths were heavily beat down and tracks were everywhere. Not only were there foot tracks, but there were also a lot of bicycle tracks. The usage of the paths was so heavy that we felt pretty sure that there would be very few booby traps to worry about.

We made the first enemy contact, around 14:00 hours in the afternoon. Our point man had smelled rice cooking and we halted until he could go up ahead and check it out. Sure enough, there were about eight gooks having lunch up ahead. We radioed Hawkeye team the situation and told them to stay put until we let them know that it was safe to proceed. We moved in and took them out. They only got off a few shots at us and nobody was hit. We destroyed their weapons and supplies and checked the bodies for any important papers. I guess they were just a careless recon team that was waiting to set up a night ambush. We moved out again and radioed Hawkeye team to do the same. Later that afternoon we were shot at by a sniper. He waited until about half the squad had passed by him, and then he started to shoot. This allowed our squad to form a semicircle around him and heat up his perch. He was in a tree that wasn't very well hidden. Luckily, he was a really bad shot and we got him before he did any damage. He looked like an old farmer and was shooting a worn out maeuser of some sort. It probably wouldn't shoot straight and that would explain why he didn't hit one of us, with his first few shots. He only had a few more rounds of ammo on him. We moved ahead and set up a night ambush site. Hawkeye team did the same, back where they were at.

When nighttime comes in the jungle, you find out what pitchblack darkness is all about. You can't even see your buddy who is sitting next to you. It is amazing how the jungle comes alive with different sounds after the sun has gone down. Our clothes were wet from the misting rain. We itched all over but couldn't scratch, because we had to be still and quiet. When you're on watch, you are scared to death and your mind will play tricks with your imagination. You hear and see things that don't really exist. When it is your turn to get some sleep, you are totally exhausted but everything is fighting to keep you awake. The rain doesn't seem to let up and the leeches will crawl on any part of your body that is not covered. It is a constant struggle to keep all the critters off of you. We all had a miserable and mostly sleepless night, but at least we did not have any surprise visits from the Viet Cong. The other squad had also been graced with a safe and quiet night. We ate our C-rations and moved out a little after daybreak, with Hawkeye trailing us.

I was given the honor of walking in the point man position this morning. I had done it many times before, so it wasn't any big deal. Both teams set out at a steady pace. It was still misting rain and we were in for another miserable day. We began to see an occasional monkey in the treetops, and we had scurried up several other forms of wildlife. I had expected to see a lot of snakes in this area, but so far we had not run across any. The fog was a little less dense today, but there were still a few patches, here and there. Our path had been paralleling a stream most of the morning. We had found two sites where gooks had prepared a morning meal, so we knew that we were not alone in this area. I give a raised fist, hand signal, to halt the patrol. The squad leader came forward to find out what the problem was. I told him that I could hear some voices up ahead. He instructed me to take another man and go check out the voices. He radioed Hawkeye team to stop until he called them back with instructions. Cpl. Morales and I moved slowly forward down the path. The voices were getting louder and louder. We eased off the pathway and worked our way to the flank of the voices. In front of us, there was a spot cleared out along the stream and they appeared to have a temporary re-supply point set up. The guerilla soldiers in this area would come through and get supplies, like rice rations and ammunition. It was sort of like a buffet service. There was probably about a dozen or more VC around the supplies. We went back and reported to our squad leader. He decided to bring the other team up and we would hit them as a mass unit, and maybe none of the enemy would get away. We took up our positions off the side of the path, and waited for the Hawkeye team. It took them about fifteen minutes to get to our location.

After the other group reached us, we all received our instructions and began to move forward. We would form a semicircle around the area, before we moved in close to open fire. The little rascals put up a pretty good fight, considering that we had them outnumbered 3 to 1 and we had hit them with an element of surprise. Two of our guys were wounded in the confrontation. One was shot in the arm and the other one had a piece shot off his ear, about the size of a dime. Both were taken care of by the medic and did not require an evac-helicopter to be brought in. There was a good assortment of supplies at this site. They had homemade tables set up in a line, with all kinds of things on each table. They had a few AK-47 assault rifles and some SKS semi-automatic rifles, a couple RPGs (rocket-propelled grenades), ammunition, rice, and even a few assorted cans of U.S. Army C-rations. All the supplies were covered with badly worn tarps to protect them from the rain. We destroyed everything with C-4 and grenades. Our squad leader said that they would probably be receiving more supplies during the night, and also some VC might come into the area for extra supplies. He said that we would be setting up two ambush sites for a welcoming party. Hawkeye team was sent back down the path to the south about 400 meters to set up their position, and Zebra would do the same to the north. We figured to see a few stragglers during the day, but most of the activity would take place after dark. Charlie was well known for their moving around at night. The two teams were close enough to hear each other's gunshots, but far enough apart, so that they would not hit each other if a bullet went astray. We could also monitor each other's activities by radio, and move in quickly if the need arose. We set up our positions, ate some chow, and settled down for a long wait.

The wait really wasn't very long. We heard voices coming, after about forty-five minutes. Two VC soldiers came casually strolling down the path. They were conversing with each other and didn't seem to have a care in the world. I'm not sure what happened, but just after they entered our kill zone, something spooked one of them and they turned to run. It was too late, because a couple of our guys opened up and they both hit the ground. The bodies were dragged into the forest and the area was restored, as much as it could be, to hide the tracks and blood. Hawkeye team was relayed the information and we settled back in again. Hawkeye team made the next contact. A lone gook came down the path on a bicycle. The squad tried to take him alive but he refused to go down without a fight, and was killed. We received word of this incident by radio. It was now getting dark, so we divided up our watch schedules.

It was probably after midnight before we heard anything other than the normal jungle noises. We began to hear some metallic clicking sounds in the distance. It was obviously headed in our direction. We woke everyone up and Hawkeye was radioed and told to be ready, in case we needed them to head in our direction quickly. The sounds were still in the distance, but we weren't sure how far. Our squad leader felt sure that it was a supply train, but didn't know what kind or how big. He wished that he had moved Hawkeye team ahead to link up with us, but it was too late now. We were told to hold our fire until the last of the supply train was within our kill zone. If the first ones passed us by, then maybe Hawkeye would get them down the path. Our nerves were jerking, because the sounds were real loud now and they were just around a bend in the path. We could see the flickering of their lights as they neared. This was really a ghostly sight in the rain and fog. I would like to have seen Pfc Hargrove's face right now. He would probably need a changing of clothes in a few minutes. The procession entered our view and we were all amazed. It was a combination of gooks carrying baskets of rice on their heads, two wheeled carts pulled by water buffalo. The carts were filled with boxes of ammunition and other assorted weaponry and supplies. Everyone had weapons but their main security source was four gooks on bicycles, with AK-47 assault rifles. Two of them were leading the convoy and the other two were bringing up the rear. The sounds we had heard were coming from the chains hooking the carts to the water buffalo. The sight was almost comical. There were several carts in the line and they were stretched out for a long way. We would have to let the two lead guards and maybe one cart pass before we could open fire.

Finally, the timing was right and we began to pick them off. It was sort of like an old-fashioned turkey shoot. We took out most of them but a few headed down the path, toward Hawkeye team. In just a moment, we heard a blast of gunfire and knew that they had made contact. They had taken out the two lead bicycle guards but a couple of rice haulers had thrown down their baskets and escaped through the forest. It would serve no purpose for us to try and chase them through the night. Neither team had taken any hits. The other squad joined up with us and we spent the remainder of the night destroying weapons and supplies. One of the water buffaloes had been killed in the firefight so we cooked steaks for breakfast.

Everyone in Vietnam knew that we were in this area now, so there was no reason for us to stay here any longer. We were ordered to leave the path and proceed to some hill to the west. Most of the hills in this country had names or numbers, but I can't remember which one it was. It was supposed to be famous for some previous battle that had taken place. That still didn't narrow it down very much.

We combined the teams and set out on another recon patrol, to our new assigned destination. It would take us the better part of the day to get there. The hump was rough but totally uneventful. We were all exhausted, but we still had to set up a night ambush, at the base of the hill. If everything went as planned, we would be airlifted out of here early the next morning. There were no fresh signs of the enemy around this area, so we felt pretty good. We would spend the night at 50% watch, so maybe we would be able to get a little sleep. We settled in for the night and things were looking real good, because it had even stopped raining.

Around 23:00 hours, the squad leader sent word down the perimeter line for us to go on one hundred percent alert. He said that something was going on out there, because everything had got to quiet. When the normal night sounds of a jungle get silent, there is something unwanted moving around in the area.

It was probably more than an hour before we heard it the first time. I'm not exactly sure how to explain what I had heard. It was sort of like someone who was very sick trying to clear their throat. The sound seemed to be moving up and down our perimeter line and we must have heard it about a half-dozen times. We were stretched out in a line perimeter, around the base of the hill and we probably covered a distance of one and a half football field lengths. The sound was beginning to change. It now sounded more like a snarl or a growl and was getting louder. Whatever was making the noise seemed to be getting mad. By now, it was obvious to everyone that the sound was not coming from a human being. We began to whisper among ourselves, and discuss the possibilities of what was out there in the dark. At one point, the sound seemed very close to where I was lying. I remember thinking to myself, *I sure hope that he has already eaten today.* It was too dark for us to see anything, and this seemed to go on forever. The sound moved away from me and continued down the perimeter line. Way down the line, a trip-flare was set off and the guys near that position reported a large striped tiger running into the forest. I never actually saw it myself, but that must have been the truth. We all stayed up the rest of the night and popped an occasional parachute flare, to illuminate the area. I don't think that we even considered the possibility of VC, in the area. We could hardly wait for the choppers to get us out of that crazy place. We were finally picked up, at about 9:00 o'clock the next morning.

When we arrived back at the base camp, we began to tell our story. Some of them laughed, but others believed us. One recon unit that had been based out of here for several months told of stories and sightings of real live Asian Bengal tigers in and around the A Shau Valley region. I would like to have seen the tiger, but not bad enough to go through another night like that one. The mission had been a very successful one. We were able to eliminate about two dozen gooks and destroy a tremendous amount of enemy weapons and supplies. We had no American soldiers killed and only two had been slightly wounded. It also gave us a memory that we would take to our graves. This was just one more saga about the A Shau Valley.

CHAPTER 13

JUNGLES REALLY DO EXIST

The closest I had ever come to a jungle, was watching a Tarzan movie on the television. Now, I was only a few minutes away from being lowered into one from a helicopter. We would have to repel a couple hundred feet down a rope, through the treetops to reach the jungle floor. I have already had the opportunity to repel on several occasions and enjoyed it very much, but this one was going to be a lot different. We would not be able to see the ground below, and we had no idea what would be waiting on us down there. I didn't know what order we would be told to exit the chopper, but somehow I was gonna try not to be first.

The pilot yelled for us to get ready, because we were within minutes of the departure point. Even the words departure point didn't sound good. We were told to lock and load our weapons prior to leaving the chopper, and be prepared for anything when we hit the ground. We would be exiting the chopper at three to five minute intervals. The first man out would anchor the bottom end of the rope with his body weight. This would help the rest of us, with a smoother ride down. As each of us hit the ground, we would take up battle positions and form a small perimeter around the anchor man. Soldiers making a rope insertion were usually not attacked until several were on the ground.

Each of us was loaded down with rations and gear. We were each carrying, between 45 and 60 pounds of equipment. I was proud to be carrying my lightweight M-16 rifle, instead of an M 60 machine gun. There was quiet a difference in the weight. We had been warned of a possible two- or three-week mission, so we were instructed to bring along certain items. Our clothing needs consisted of several pairs of socks, several pairs of underwear, one changing of our shirt and trousers, and a poncho. Our normal recon supplies were weapons and their cleaning gear, entrenching tools, survival knives, ammo, assorted grenades, mines, flares, radios, first-aid kits, maps, compasses, flashlights, batteries, detonators, wire, rope, foot powder, water, mirrors, food rations, and mosquito nets. Personal items were optional and could be such things as: soap, toothbrush, toothpaste, comb, razor, and writing materials. Personal hygiene sometimes was impossible. We tried to brush our teeth every few days, and shaving and bathing were done when time and conditions permitted. I know that it is disgusting to say such a thing, but a person actually gets used to stinking and being filthy. I didn't say that he likes it, but he can learn to tolerate it. When you stink yourself, you don't seem to notice the others around you.

There had been several guys go down before me, so at least that prayer had been answered. As I started repelling down the rope, my mind began filling with thoughts of bad things that were waiting for me at the bottom. When I entered the treetops, I had to work my way between the dense growths of limbs. My equipment and weapons were trying to hang up on everything. I feared that some of my equipment would be ripped from me, and I knew that would not make the anchor man very happy. I could form a picture of everything falling and hitting him on the head. When I broke through the limbs,

I figured that I had clear sailing ahead. I looked down and saw that there was another layer of limb canopy that was thicker than the one I had just fought my way through. I started the same ordeal again, and finally slipped to the jungle floor beside my comrades. I ran to a spot and took up my battle position in the forming perimeter.

There were five chopper loads of soldiers who were unloading at the same time. All of this was taking place in an area no bigger than two football fields. Once everyone was safely on the ground, we would rally together and receive our next orders.

The insertion had taken place late in the afternoon and had only taken a few minutes. I can't say that it was done quietly, because we made a good bit of noise coming down through the trees. Our ranking man on this mission would be Master Sergeant Phillip Sanders. Everyone called him Papa Phil, because he was twice as old as most of us. He was a highly decorated war veteran and we were pleased to be serving under his command. After we all came together, he informed us that we had lost one man in the helicopter insertion. He had broken a leg when he hit some of the limbs. He was hooked back to the rope and hauled back up, out of the jungle.

Our mission was to work our way through the jungle to a predetermined area that was going to serve as a temporary firebase. Another unit was already at the area awaiting our arrival. We would be serving as security for that unit, while they cleared and erected the fire-base. They were receiving a lot of enemy resistance that we encountered along the way. Papa Phil divided us into three squads and assigned our line positions. Each squad would consist of ten to twelve members. We would move through the jungle in a line formation. There would be a center squad, with one on each of their flanks. The position of the squad would be rotated, throughout the day. Our recon goal was to search out and destroy any enemy troops along the way. Intelligence reports warned us of a heavy concentration of enemy activity between us and our intended destination. It looked like we would be earning our money on this mission.

We were instructed to break up into our squads and be prepared to move out in ten minutes. We would only be patrolling a short time today, because it was about one hour till sundown. I didn't see what difference it would make when the sun went down, because this place was always dark. Very little sunlight was able to get through two dense layers of tree limbs and vegetation. It was unbelievable how thick the canopies were. The patrolling should be reasonably easy because there was very little underbrush or low-growing limbs. Our main obstacles would be the abundance of tree trunks. The floor of the jungle was covered by a two or three inch layer of moss. It looked and felt like a soft carpet. This sure beat humping across rocks and hard ground. There was a mist in the air, and a heavy fog was trying to set in, yet it was extremely hot because there was no air circulation at all. I felt like I was in a trance, as we began to move out.

We moved slowly and cautiously, as we let our eyes and minds adjust to the surroundings. We had only been walking about 45 minutes when Papa Phil called a halt. He felt that this was the perfect spot to set up our night bivouac area. One guy patted the mossy ground cover and commented that he was looking forward to a good night's sleep on this heavenly mattress. Papa Phil cautioned us to cover the moss with our poncho liners, before we sat down or lay down. He said that under the moss, was infested with critters that we didn't want to know about. This sort of put a cramp on a good night.

We set up a circular perimeter. Two men were placed on each position, so that we could rotate sleeping every two hours. This would give us fifty percent alertness at all times. Each position was responsible to put out their trip flares, claymore mines and any other little surprises for Charlie. It was surprising how dark it became when the sun had totally gone down. I couldn't tell if the moon was out or not. The fog was real thick and you could feel it more than see it. As things began to settle down, the night critters began to serenade us with all kinds of sounds. There were even several varieties of night birds that began to converse with each other. They were probably laughing at the human dummies lying around on their jungle floor. Other than the bug bites that we had to endure, the night crept by uneventfully. I don't know of anybody that got much sleep, except for Papa Phil. He swore that he had slept like a baby.

We had breakfast, just as the sun was coming up, and we set out shortly after we finished. We were able to cover a lot of ground and didn't have any problems, till we broke for lunch. We had guards posted and the rest of us were sitting around discussing the morning. A little breeze had picked up this morning and we had made it pretty good. There were lots of colorful birds and the vegetation was spectacular. We had seen two cobras and one small python, so it was obvious to everyone that snakes were plentiful in this area.

Suddenly, a series of several shots were fired at us. It was obvious that they were coming from more than one direction. We all dove for cover behind trees and things. One of the snipers were spotted quickly and taken out by an M-60 machine gun. He fell like a ton of bricks from the top of a large tree. The other one decided to retreat and dropped about fifteen feet from the limb of another tree. He was spotted immediately, and was also killed. They had managed to shoot one of our guys, but it was only a flesh wound in his upper left arm. He said it wasn't a big deal, because he shot with his right arm. We felt sure that these were the only two snipers. The bodies were checked for documents and other items. Their weapons and ammo was destroyed with a frag grenade. We radioed in about the two KIA-VC and were informed to leave the bodies and continue with our mission. Papa Phil said that the two snipers had probably been following us all day and were waiting for us to take a break, so they could pick some of us off. Lucky for us, it didn't turn out the way they had planned.

We started out patrolling again, keeping a safe but respectable pace. We made it through the entire afternoon without any enemy contact, but there was plenty of sign to let us know that a lot of recent activity had taken place in this area. I told one of my buddies that I had felt like someone was watching us the entire afternoon. He had felt the same thing.

We had covered a lot of ground today, and were all exhausted. After setting up night perimeter, we had a little light left to do things like eat and write letters. The first priority of most was to clean their weapon. Even though most of us had not fired our weapon today, we still broke it down and cleaned it. A little unwanted dirt and grime could cause a malfunction and possibly cost us our lives. Papa Phil said that we did not have to worry about silence, because he felt real sure that Charlie knew exactly where we were at. Most of us still held the conversation to a minimum and we tried to stay as still as possible. You could feel the tenseness in the air. Night came and we prepared for the worst.

It has been my experience that most night attacks occur during the wee hours of the morning. I guess the enemy figures that you will be slower to react and more vulnerable during these hours. There was one advantage to our location. The heavy tree canopy above us would keep the gooks from lobbing mortars onto our locations. They will have to attack us head-on, and that would at least give us targets to shoot at. I spent my first two hours on guard, trying to focus on good things. My mind flashed back to the many good times that I had during my childhood and school years, and then I began to think about my girlfriend. I had a gorgeous girl and missed her dearly. I lied a lot in my letters to her, and she was unaware of most of the bad things that I had experienced over here. I heard a twig snap and my mind was jerked back into reality. I decided that I had better focus my thoughts on surviving one more night in Vietnam.

It seemed like I had just fallen asleep, when my bubby bumped my leg and whispered that there was movement outside our perimeter. I could see that a trip-flare had been detonated about three positions down from ours. The flare had hung up in the tree canopy and was causing weird, ghostlike silhouettes to dance across the jungle floor. We began to receive small arms fire from all over the place. According to the accuracy of these shots, it was obvious that they knew where most of our guard locations were. We were all dug in, behind logs and things, so we were pretty safe for the moment. Other flares began to go off, so we knew that they were advancing on our positions. This meant that we would have to expose ourselves from behind the safety of our logs, but we had no choice. A couple of guys had detonated a claymore mine, and it was obvious by the yells that the timing had been perfect. We had no way to evaluate the size of the enemy force, but we were sure that there were plenty to go around. The battle was raging on all sides now. Screams of pain and agony were coming from inside and outside our perimeter. The battle continued for a long time, but we were holding our ground and it was apparent that the enemy was moving away from our positions. We kept receiving occasional harassment fire until daylight, but the battle was definitely over. Papa Phil sent out some advance observers, to make sure that the enemy was gone and our dangers were past. We had only lost one man in battle and had two wounded: one minor and one severely. We called in an airlift for our KIA and WIA. They had to be hauled back up through the tree canopies. The minor wound was treated on site. The enemy count was 16 KIA and the wounded were either dragged away by their buddies, or managed to crawl away on their own. There were several blood trails leading off into the jungle. Our spirits were pretty high, but we were saddened by the loss of our fellow soldiers. We moved out as soon as the airlift was completed.

The morning passed by smoothly. There was still a lot of enemy sign, but no one spotted any VC. The underbrush was beginning to get denser, and this worried us a great deal. This meant more places for Charlie to hide, and ambush us from. They knew exactly where we were going, and the areas that we would have to cover to get there.

We hadn't eaten since yesterday, and it didn't look like we would be stopping for lunch. Papa Phil overheard one GI complaining; he laughed and told him that he could eat when we got to our destination tomorrow. This guy was new in country and didn't realize that this was normal for a recon patrol.

We were told to halt and take a break, while Papa Phil received more orders on the radio. He said that the fire-base crew was getting pounded pretty hard, and the VC was trying to overrun them before we could arrive and reinforce them. Papa Phil was able to talk directly to the commanding officer of the fire-base. He doubted if they would be able to hang on through the night. We were not scheduled to arrive there until around noon tomorrow. We did not have enough daylight left today, to make it to our destination, even with cooperation from the enemy. Papa Phil was told that our orders would not allow us to continue after dark. Papa Phil explained the situation to us, and said that we needed to be fully alert, because we were going to cover as much ground as possible before nightfall. We set out at a good rapid pace. We ran into resistance several times that afternoon, but it was always from snipers in trees. We were usually able to locate and take them out rather quickly and continue our quest forward. We encountered several booby traps along the way, but somehow were able to bypass them without harm. We did end up losing two more soldiers that afternoon from the snipers. We decided to bag the bodies and take them with us. The airlifts would have used up a lot of valuable time.

We halted just prior to the end of the day and Papa Phil gathered us up for a powwow. He told us that we were about three hard hours from our destination. He wanted to know how we felt about going on in tonight. He said that he would leave the decision up to a vote. I never heard of that happening in the Army. Phil gave us a pep talk, and bragged on us about our performance thus far. He said that he knew that we were tired and hungry, but our fellow soldiers needed us badly. He explained the added dangers of night movement in these conditions, and said that we might run into something that was too big for us to handle. The vote was unanimous and all voted to move forward. Papa Phil said that he needed to radio in and tell them our intentions.

It was very obvious, what he had been told on the radio. They had told him to stop for the night, and he knew that he would not be able to live with himself if he obeyed those orders. He also knew that he might be court marshaled for not obeying them. He was a career soldier and his entire future could depend on this decision. He sure didn't seem to spend much time thinking about it. He started yelling that we would be observing total radio silence during our night movement, and would contact them again from our final destination point. He hung the radio receiver up and calmly said, "Let's move out and save our buddies." We all looked at him with awe, and then jumped to obey his orders.

We hit the trail again. This time we seemed to have much more spirit and determination about our objective. I was swelled with pride to know that I was serving with Papa Phil Sanders. The mission outcome was still unsure but we would definitely do our best. I wondered if the court-marshal would filter down to each of us, ha.

Apparently, the enemy did not think that we were crazy enough to move at night, so they were totally unprepared. As we stomped through the jungle, we received occasional small arms fire from gooks who were retreating from our path. We would return fire and keep marching. About two hours into our trek, we came upon a VC bivouac site. Our point man had spotted them in advance, and we were able to attack them before they knew we were there. We killed thirteen and a couple were able to get away in the dark jungle. We had to take time to destroy their weapons and search them for valuable documents. This took longer than we wanted. We finished and took off again. Our radio had been turned off by Papa Phil, so no communication had taken place. We did not even report this skirmish.

We were close enough now to our destination that we could hear the exchange of gunfire between the two forces. We hoped and prayed that we would not be too late.

Radio silence was broke and we told the camp commander that we had about 15 minutes out and would be coming in from the east. We would be popping illumination flares and red smoke for identification. Papa Phil said that the man was crying on the other end of the radio. We entered the area with guns blazing and the gooks took off, like the true cowards that they are. I guess they had no way of knowing the size of our force. We re-captured the compound at 11 o'clock that night.

We were greeted with a hero's welcome. We received cheers and pats on the back from everyone. It looked like a family reunion of folks that had not seen each other for a long time. The camp had held up well, since the sun went down, but they were low on ammo. Some gooks had already entered the perimeter. It was only a matter of time before they would have been overrun.

We rotated guard assignments and everyone tried to get some well-deserved sleep. I don't think that anyone even bothered to eat until the next morning. We were able to receive an ammo, rations, and water air drop the next day. We spent another 16 days at this camp, and supplied them with adequate security. We received daily harassment fire. But that was all. The local residents were able to construct the necessary facilities and get the camp ready for normal operations. From this point on, there would be a steady flow of recon units dropping by for a little rest and recuperation.

I never did hear what name was given to this fire-base. Nothing was ever done about Papa Phil's court-marshal and I never had the privilege of serving with him again.

Chapter 14

INEXPERIENCE CAN BE DEADLY

It had turned out to be another boring patrol. This was our third day in the bush, and we were all eager to return to our base camp. A hot meal and a shower would be a welcome change. We would be arriving at our pickup point in about six hours. Our orders for this mission had been short and sweet, and everything was scheduled to go uneventfully. We were to patrol sector Delta and look for any signs that would signify that there had been any enemy activity in this area recently. Thus far, we had not seen anything that would make us think that this was true.

Our recon squad was made up of fourteen members and eight of them were fairly new in country. Several of them had never seen any action or been in a real firefight. Our squad leader had been instructed to treat this as a training mission and act like we were expecting to make enemy contact at any moment. I had learned a long time ago that each and every mission should be treated like that. The new men would get an opportunity to feel some of the pressure, without actually getting shot at.

The last couple of nights had been spent, in well-guarded bivouac sites. We had been told to dig two-man foxholes, and we were to rotate our sleeping shifts every two hours. We surrounded our perimeter with flares and claymore mines. During the middle of the second night a couple of the new guys reported that they had heard some movement in the bushes, but I felt sure that it was just their imaginations, or maybe some small critters moving around out there. Vietnam was definitely known for all sorts of wildlife. We checked the area real good the next morning and there were no signs of enemy presence during the night. One of the new guys had only been in Vietnam for about two weeks. His name was Private First Class John Whitaker and he was from some place down in Texas. He was one of those fellows who thought he knew everything. He was real cocky and didn't seem to understand that his job was very dangerous. He seemed to think that it was just a game. He kept telling us that he had done all of this stuff, back in A.I.T. He was only nineteen years old, but that wasn't so unusual, because so was I. Everything that our squad leader told him to do, was treated as a joke and questioned with a debate. He was continually making fun of the enemy and saying that they were no match for his cunning wit and training.

I had been assigned the task of walking point on this particular mission. I had been in country for almost eight months and the squad leader had true confidence in my ability to sense danger. I had a pretty good eye for seeing anything that was unusual or out of place. Private Whitaker had been a real pest all day and wanted the squad leader to let him take over the point-man position.

We stopped for a short break and the squad leader flagged me to come over and have a talk with him. He wanted to know what I thought about letting Whitaker take the lead. I told him that it was his call, but I felt like we were in a real safe area. I had not seen anything for the last two and a half days and I wasn't expecting to now. We decided to give him a try. At least, maybe it would shut him up for a while. We also discussed the possibility of shooting him, but that probably wasn't the best option right now. I gave Whitaker a ten-minute briefing on what he should be watching out for, but I doubt if he heard a word that I had said to him.

We started back on patrol again. He signaled us forward, like we were in the cavalry. We were patrolling in a double column staggered formation. Private Whitaker took the point position and I dropped back about twenty feet and slipped into the slackman slot. The terrain was fairly clear and I had a good view of Whitaker. We had only moved a couple hundred yards when the whole world seemed to explode in front of me. Private Whitaker had literally disintegrated before me. I removed parts of his body from my uniform. The rest of the squad automatically went into a combat defensive position until I could move up and check out the situation. It appeared that the highly trained Private Whitaker had stepped onto an anti-personnel mine. It had detonated when his body weight pushed down on top of the mine. It was very unusual for an anti-personnel mine to have this much explosive capability. It was designed to maim or kill a person, but not blow them into tiny pieces. The mine had probably been there for several months.

We put the parts that we were able to find, in a body bag and would take it with us. Most of the new guys were throwing up over in the bushes. Needless to say, I took back over the point position for the remainder of the trip. I'm not sure who took it harder, the squad leader or me. I felt real bad about volunteering to shoot him. We both knew that our superiors would not be pleased with our decision, allowing him to take the point. This was supposed to be an uneventful patrol and we would be returning with a full body bag. At least the other guys had learned that Vietnam was a very dangerous duty assignment. Direct contact with Charlie, was not the only dangers over here.

We were able to make it back to our pickup point by the originally scheduled time. I had speeded up our pace a little, to make up for the time that we had lost. We loaded onto the choppers and they took us back to our base camp. We did enjoy warm meals and showers that night, but all of our minds were on other things. The brass wasn't too happy with our squad leader, but it was just another casualty of war. I will always wonder if that mine was really meant for me, and would my combat experiences have saved my life. God works in mysterious ways

CHAPTER 15

ANOTHER DAY AT THE OFFICE

The sun was beating down on us as we humped through a small valley between two large hills. Our bodies and uniforms were totally soaked with sweat. We had already been out here for three days, so we had got used to the stench of each other. It is hard to imagine but you stop noticing the smell, after the first couple of days. The only water sources that we had ran across were stagnant and useless for personal hygiene purposes. The water in our canteens was much too precious, to be wasted on such trivial matters. The last three days we had been through some areas that were supposed to be densely populated with VC regular troops, but somehow we had failed to make contact with any of them.

Our mission was an ordinary search and destroy reconnaissance that was scheduled to last about ten days. We humped through the bush all day, and set up ambush sites at night. Most of the terrain had not been extremely bad, but we had crossed through a dense section of elephant grass yesterday and the razor-sharp blades had opened up some pretty nasty cuts on a couple of the guys. The continuous sweating and filth of our bodies could easily turn these cuts into some really serious infectious sores. I had a few minor cuts myself, but none were very serious. The salt in a person's sweat will keep an open wound irritated and makes them feel like they are on fire. Our team medic was constantly checking us for fever and signs of infection. A good medic, serving in the fields of Vietnam, was worth his weight in gold. I have witnessed on many occasions where a medic would put his own butt on the line to give aid to a wounded team member. Most of them did not have a medical background, but were ran through some quickie first-aid classes and the rest was learned from on-the-job training. Even their bag of medical supplies was very limited, but they still did an outstanding job, tending to a hurt soldier, until they could be airlifted out of harm's way. During the wee morning hours of our fourth night in the field, we heard several Vietnamese voices outside the ambush perimeter. They seemed to be fairly close but we could not see them and they never set off any of our trip-flares or booby traps. The voices only stayed in the vicinity for a short time, and then we heard them fade into the night. It was quiet for the remainder of the night. When the sun came up, we went out and found signs and tracks, to support their presence. They had stomped all around one of the trip-flares and I do not understand why it was never set off. It appeared that there must have been about a halfdozen of them. The fifth day promised to be a real scorcher. One of the team members had a small transistor radio and he had been listening to a local station. The broadcaster said that the temperature would probably reach around 118 degrees Fahrenheit today. Needless to say, we were all excited about another day of humping in the heat. Anytime that we were able to stop for a brief rest, we would wipe down our weapons and try to keep them from any sweat and grime. No matter what condition our bodies were in, our main concern was taking care of our weapons, because our very lives could depend on its reliability. Even though we had an assortment of C-rations, they all start to taste the same after several days in the bush. We all had one changing of our outer uniform but we had not utilized the second pair yet. We had several changes of underwear and tried to rotate them every few days. This would at least allow them to dry from the sweat and cut down on chaffing. The most important part of a grunt's body is his feet. We used a lot of foot powder and tried to change our socks daily, even though it meant using dirty ones over and over again. Jungle rot was a major problem that the American combat soldier had to face in Vietnam. Most of us had a case of it and there was no way to get rid of it. Sometimes the skin on the bottom of our feet would bubble up and when these bubbles would burst, we had to contend with large raw places that bled continuously. The blood would dry and stick to the socks, so when we took them off, some raw meat would usually come off with them. We had to train our minds to forget about the pain, because the next day would usually bring more hills to climb and more clicks to hump. Our minds had to stay alert, to the surroundings and any possible dangers that were lurking down the next path.

Our first enemy contact occurred around mid morning of the sixth day of this mission. We were entering another small valley, when we started to receive small arms fire from one of the hillsides. We all dove for cover and waited a few moments before peeking out. An occasional clump of dirt would be kicked up by a bullet hitting the ground nearby. There were a lot of big rocks to hide behind, so we were all secure for the moment. It was obvious that a couple of snipers had been placed on the side of the hill, as a welcoming party to any unsuspecting recon squad that entered their firing zone. I heard one of the team members say that, at least we were getting to rest for a while. If it had been near nightfall, we would probably have waited them out and moved out under the cover of darkness, but we had a lot of daylight hours left, so we would have to make our move soon to keep other enemy troops from coming to the sounds of a firefight. We had located the positions of the two snipers, so we laid down a barrage of heavy fire to keep their heads down, while a couple of our team members flanked them on each side. This worked perfect and our men were able to slip around and take them out. After destroying their weapons and supplies, we hit the trail again. The whole thing had not taken more than forty-five minutes. We located and destroyed several booby traps later that afternoon. We set up our night ambush and it passed by quietly.

Day seven started out the same way as the others. The entire morning would be spent making a torturous climb up the side of a steep hill. The underbrush had become a lot thicker and we were having to hack our way through some of the stuff with our machetes. We would try to reach the summit by mid afternoon and this would give us the remainder of the daylight hours to observe the low lying areas that surrounded the hill. By the time we reached the summit, we were all totally exhausted. We found a band of orangutans that had set up house on the top of this hill. We were able to drive them away with our machetes and some rocks. We didn't want to fire any shots, if we could help it. It was around 14:00 hours, by this time.

We divided up into pairs and spread out to observe the area below us. We broke out some C-rations and enjoyed a leisurely meal. Our squad leader told us that we could take turns sleeping, if one of us was alert at all times. He suggested that we go ahead and set up our night positions, because we would be staying here until the next morning. The squad had a couple of pair of binoculars and we were able to see VC movement in three different areas. One group was a small recon unit, moving down a path in the valley below. They were moving away from us and did not pose any threat to our team. They were too far away for us to shoot at them. The second visual movement was three gooks carrying baskets of rice on their heads. They were probably going to meet up with a recon unit that needed some food rations. The third group was the one that interested all of us. It appeared to be a large bivouac site, about three quarters of a mile to the north of our location. We estimated that there were seventy-five or eighty VC soldiers, moving around the area presently. They must be building up their numbers for something special. We radioed our findings to brigade headquarters. Brigade seemed to think that a large VC defensive attack was in the making, and this was one of the areas that would be used for a troop build-up point. We were ordered to hold our positions and observe the activities, throughout the night. We were to update them on any major developments that happened during the night. Brigade would send a high-altitude surveillance plane, to take aerial photos, early the next morning. Even though we were aware of enemy presence in the near vicinity, we felt very secure on top of this hill. The VC had no reason to waste their time climbing up this big hill. We would not be putting out any trip-flares, because we didn't want an animal to set one off and give away our position.

We were more concerned about the return of the orangutans than the enemy troops. The squad leader put us on one-third alert. We had a fifteen man unit, so five men would be on watch at all times. We would pull two-hour shifts, then get to sleep for four straight hours. The five men on watch would be positioned, so that the entire surrounding area below would be in view of someone. We settled in, for what we hoped would be a restful and quiet night. The night was clear and the sky was full of stars. I was thinking about my girl back home, as I drifted off to sleep.

As dawn was breaking, we all began to stir and discuss how restful we felt this morning. It had been a long time since any of us had the opportunity to sleep four hours in a row. A couple of the team members reported that they had observed lights moving down some paths during the night, toward the enemy bivouac area. There was definitely a lot more gooks down there this morning. The sergeant radioed in and estimated the enemy build up to be at around one hundred and thirty soldiers. The surveillance was already in the air and brigade was awaiting their return, with some aerial photos. We were ordered to stay in place and continue observing the site. We had no problem with that request. We dined on a gourmet breakfast of C-rations. The extreme heat would not allow us to get any more sleep, but at least we would not be stomping around in the field all day. We voted to stay on the same watch schedule, as long as brigade told us to remain in this sector. Some of us were going to use this spare time to catch up on our letter writing, and others just lay around resting. Sarge said for us to limit our moving around and for us to stay concealed behind brush and rocks. The underbrush was extremely dense up here so that shouldn't be any problem. It wasn't very long until we got a call from brigade headquarters. The aerial photos not only confirmed our findings, but it also showed another large enemy build up site, about six miles to the east. Apparently, we were sitting smack dab in the middle of several hundred VC troops. I didn't feel quite as safe anymore. We were told to hold our positions and continue watching the enemy activities down below. They wanted to let as many VC, as possible, gather in these areas before sending in air strikes. They would be getting things ready and monitoring the VC's activities through us.

Throughout the morning, we observed a few more stragglers join the ranks of the enemy. We began to get bored with our surroundings and were actually looking forward to moving out again. As the day drug on, it became obvious that the gooks were preparing to depart the area real soon. They were getting their individual gear together and they seemed to be dividing into squad size groups for their final instructions. We radioed to brigade that it was probably time for them to make their move. They said the planes were waiting on standby and would be off the ground in minutes.

They had already plotted their grid co-ordinances for the bombing runs, and were ready to rock and roll. Their estimated time of arrival at our location was approximately twenty-three minutes. Most of that time would be used for the big planes to gain the proper bombing altitudes. We all gathered on that side of the hill and waited their arrival, with great anticipation. The procession was led by a B-52 bomber. He unloaded on the site with a load of explosives and napalm. The valley floor lit up with a wall of fire and the ground was trembling around us, from the bombs exploding. They must have decided to hit both enemy areas at the same time. We could hear the explosions and see the smoke billowing upward, in an area to our east. A couple of fighter jets followed the B-52 and proceeded to induce much more destruction to the area. The back door of the assault was closed by some Cobra assault helicopters. They penetrated the area with mini-gun bursts and made several loops, sweeping the surrounding areas. This was the most amazing thing that I had ever witnessed. The aircraft disappeared in the distance and it was all over. I knew that it could not be possible for any living thing, to have survived such a deadly assault. We could smell the napalm in the hot humid air.

We radioed brigade and attempted to explain what we had just witnessed but the proper words were hard to find. They told us that the photo footage of this air assault would be sent back to the States for news broadcasting. If this did not impress the American public about our war capabilities, then nothing would.

They wanted us to enter the area and check it out, but not until the next morning. They felt like, any VC that may have escaped the attack would be running around the sector, and this would give them plenty of time to leave the area. There would be choppers observing the area, for the rest of the afternoon and this should assure us that the gooks would depart the area, prior to our entry in the morning.

Another recon unit would be brought in, to check out the other location to our east. We were not looking forward to the next morning. The heat and the humidity would cause the bodies to start decaying more quickly. The vultures would start arriving at daybreak and the stench would be unbearable. We settled down for our eighth night in the bush. There were still fires burning where the napalm had torched the area.

The night dragged by and I wasn't able to get very much sleep. I kept having nightmares of battlefields of days gone by. I could plainly see the faces of buddies who had been killed, and the dead enemy bodies strewn around. I dreaded the next day but I was also glad, when the daylight began to pierce the horizon. I think that I had rather be facing a firefight than to face what we would find down below.

We were not in any hurry to get started, but the sergeant suggested that none of us eat breakfast, for obvious reasons, so we grabbed our gear and hit the trail. We figured that our appetites would not be a problem, for the rest of this day. I slid into the point-man position, as we moved out. The sarge said that it would take us several hours to reach the site, because of the denseness of the underbrush. We would have to hack a path as we descended the hill. The heat was extreme and our water rations were getting real slim. We were assured that there would be choppers nearby, if we ran into any resistance. I didn't think that any gooks would still be in the area. They had to know that American troops would be converging on this sector real soon to check on the result of the air assault. We could smell the site well before we actually entered it. The smell of napalm was still heavy in the air, but the dominant odor was that of burned human flesh. This is a smell that a person can never forget. A couple of the team members were already beginning to gag. We began to enter the area where all the brush and trees were burned or charred. My body started to tense up and horror filled my mind.

As we entered the main bivouac area, I was not prepared for the horrible sight in front of me. I threw up like a dog, and most of the other team members did also. Body parts were scattered in every direction. It would have been impossible to even estimate an accurate body count. After we got our composure together, we began to search for wounded survivors, but we knew that we would not find any. I'm not even sure if there was one whole complete dead body in this mess. Everything in this area was charred from the napalm. Even the exposed ground was scorched. All their weapons, ammunition, and other supplies were destroyed beyond recognition. There were still a few stumps and logs burning in the area. We radioed in our findings and requested to leave this location as soon as possible. Apparently, the reports from the other enemy bivouac area were about the same as this one. An engineering battalion would be brought in to dig a mass grave, for all the bodies. Their families would probably never know what really happened to them. Maybe that would be a good thing.

We were airlifted out a few hours later, when the engineering battalion arrived on the scene. We returned to base camp for a couple of days and the whole routine started over. Even though we were not actually involved in this battle, I will have to live with its results for the rest of my life.

CHAPTER 16

SILENT KILL

We were being sent out on an intelligence-gathering mission. Our orders called for seven to ten days out in the bush and very little resistance and contact. This usually meant heavy and continuous fighting. They had issued cameras, sketch pads, and a tape recorder to take with us. This sounded more like a school field trip than a combat mission. We had been given very detailed grid maps of the area. They pinpointed trails, bivouac areas, streams, an old bunker complex, a couple of tunnels, and other things of interest. I had never seen a map that was quite as detailed and complex. We all had our doubts about its accuracy. We had been put in some bad situations in the past, because of incorrect maps. One of the maps was highlighted with four possible escape exits, or pickup points, if we got in over our heads and needed to be extracted quickly. These were areas where choppers had easy access to the ground and a clear spot to land. These were also good points for us to regroup, if a firefight caused us to get separated. These areas had probably been marked and cleared by another unit patrolling this region earlier.

Our mission would take place in a northern sector, of the Central Highlands. Most of the terrain was rough, but we had certainly seen a lot worse. Our squad would consist of eighteen men and we were all familiar with each other. This always seemed to help a mission go a lot smoother. We would be carrying all our essential recon gear, plus the cameras and things. Our main concern would be extra socks, underwear, and foot powder, because it was in the middle of the monsoon season and the weather would be miserable. It was raining continuously, day and night. Everything we owned would be soaked by the time we formed our squad on the ground. We were to be dropped in by chopper, and our schedule was for 06:00 hours, the next morning. This would put us on the ground, just after daybreak.

This mission was set up, because of recent reports from the air-surveillance people. We had planes that were continually flying over different sectors, to observe and take aerial photos of the ground activity. Some planes took these pictures from high altitude, and others were low flyers. The reports said that there was a lot of activity in this area, but most of it was singles or small groups of dinks. They were confused at what the gooks were planning to do. It would be our job to answer this question.

The choppers were warming up and waiting for us to board. We would be going in on three choppers. They would touch down just long enough for us to unload, and then they would zoom back in the sky, hopefully before Charlie seen them. It was obvious that the spot the choppers chose had been used before, for just such an occasion. As our feet hit the ground, we ran and dove into a prone position, near the tree line. We stayed in this position until everyone was safely on the ground. At this point, we slowly moved forward about thirty meters, into the cover of the trees. We stayed here for several minutes, without making a movement or sound. This gave us time for our eyes to focus on the surroundings and listen for any unusual sounds. All seemed to be safe and secure. Our squad leader told us to take up our positions. We had discussed the mission, prior to departing our compound, so each of us knew what position we were expected to fill. I had chosen to bring an AK-47 Chinese rifle on this mission, instead of my M-16 rifle. It was a little heavier but was a lot more dependable, in these weather conditions. It also had a lot more knock-down power. Some of the special operations units were allowed to choose the weapon they carried. The terrain here wasn't too bad, so we set out in a staggered column formation. We were told to be alert and very observant. What else is new? It was pouring down rain and we were already miserable. Oh well, it sure beat being back home sitting in a recliner and watching television, ha. We were already seeing signs of recent activity in this area. There were footprints and a place where someone had prepared a hot meal. The footprints were only a few hours old, because they had not been washed away by the heavy rain, but the meal site could be several days old. We were following a trail marked on one of the maps. We stayed off the trail and flanked each side. Our point man was one of the best in the game. He found a booby trap, so we all stopped to watch him disarm it. Of course, we give him plenty of working room. The booby trap was a grenade hooked to a piece of string. The pin had already been removed, so when someone hit the string, the grenade would be snatched loose and would detonate. He replaced the pin and put the grenade in his pack. The grenade was a U.S. issued one. We took a photo of him, disarming the grenade. I'm not sure if this would qualify as an intelligence photo, or not. We continued the rest of the day without any resistance, but saw plenty of enemy sign. The squad leader was recording all our findings on the grid maps or the tape recorder.

The second day was a little more entertaining. We located several booby traps and killed two VC who were retreating from our pathway. The signs of activity were becoming more regular. We started finding small piles of dirt that looked very suspicious. It looked like it was being dumped out of round containers. The rain was beating it down pretty good, but you could still tell, by the shape that it wasn't normal. It was never dumped on the trail, but always in the brush alongside. This was to keep it from being seen as easily. The piles seemed to be consistent in size and shape. Our findings were not only reported on paper and tape, but also had to be updated daily by radio. Everyone seemed to be totally confused about the piles of dirt.

The third day was consistent with our first one. We saw plenty of signs, but did not run into any resistance. The dirt piles continued and were being found more regularly. We had crisscrossed our sector this morning and were now following a stream that was running in the same general direction of the path that we had been following the prior two days. Oddly enough, we were still seeing the weird piles of dirt. This really threw us for a loop.

We continued moving forward on day four. We had seen three VC on a faraway hill moving away from us. The trees were thick in that area and we could only get a glimpse of them through our binoculars. Each of them seemed to be carrying a couple of buckets. This could explain how the dirt was being moved, but why? The gooks were a long way off, so we felt sure that they never saw us. About the time we reached the location, where we had seen the three VC, we found a heavily used trail leading away from the stream. We had stopped finding the piles of dirt, and this confused us even more. Our squad leader said that we would follow this trail for a while and see where it was leading to. Of course, we flanked the path, by a safe distance. We were moving slowly and quietly. After several hundred meters, we began to smell rice cooking, and our point man spotted smoke up ahead. The point man, myself, and one other soldier were sent ahead, to check the situation out. The number of booby traps was unbelievable in this area. Most of them were simple, so we disarmed them as we went. It turned out that the smoke was coming from a cook fire that was being used to prepare an evening meal. It was obvious that this area was being used for a night bivouac. The force could not be very large, because it was a small area. There were two VC preparing the meal, but after observing them for a few minutes, we re-tracked our steps back to our squad. We gave a full report of our findings to the squad leader. He radioed in our news, and our orders were to check it out further. We decided to move the whole squad in closer, because the sun would be going down in less than an hour.

We followed the same path to avoid any additional booby traps. It was very obvious what direction the Cong had been using to enter the area. We set up a line perimeter on the opposite side and waited. We were close enough to observe, but not be seen. As the sun went down, the VC began coming into the bivouac area. There seemed to be about two-dozen of them. There were even several women in the group. They had weapons, but they didn't seem to be concerned about anything. This didn't act like any fighting group that we had ever run across before. The night air was a little brisk so they had two fires going for warmth. This lit up their entire area, and we had an excellent view of them. The bugs were driving us crazy, but we couldn't move or even breathe too hard. They began to eat supper and sit around in small groups to talk. I could hear them talking, but I didn't have a clue what was being said. Occasionally, one of them would wander in our direction to take care of their bodily functions. Fortunately, they never came close enough to see us. The bad part was that we were downwind and the smell was sickening.

After about two hours, they began to settle down and get ready for sleep. Soon, everything got quiet and it was obvious that their day was over. They only left one man on guard and he didn't look too energetic. We continued to wait until we were sure that everyone was asleep. Some of them did not even have their weapons close to them. It was obvious that these guys were not used to fighting. The fires were still going and the area was well lit up. The squad leader decided that we were going to take them out, but the guard would need to be dealt with first. If he spotted us coming, then the others would be warned and we might have some American casualties. I was chosen to take out the guard. The only thing that bothered me was the brightness of the area. I applied heavy camouflage to my face and hands to cut down on the reflection of my skin against the firelight. I laid my rifle on the ground and took out my K-Bar knife. I began to crawl on my belly toward the guard. I would move a few meters, then stop. Anytime the guard was looking in my direction, I would lie perfectly still. It seemed like hours, before I was in position to make my move. The rest of the squad was ready to spring into action. The guard was standing up and leaning against a tree. He seemed to be half asleep, and his weapon was hanging loosely from his shoulder. I knew that I would need to keep his weapon from falling when I killed him. I eased up on my knees behind his tree. He was still totally unaware of my presence. I sprang upward grabbing his weapon with one hand, and used my K-Bar to cut his throat with my other hand. After a quick slicing motion, I covered his mouth and broke his neck, in one movement. I supported his weight and rifle with my other hand. A person with a cut throat can still run around and make weird noises until he finally dies. A cut throat and a broken neck will usually kill him instantly. I held on to him until I was sure that he was dead. I slowly lowered him and his weapon quietly to the ground. Suddenly, I realized that I was standing in the middle of a VC camp totally alone. I got the guard's weapon and signaled my squad to move in. It was as if the VC had been drugged, none of them had stirred at all.

My squad moved into position and opened fire on the sleeping VC. I don't think that they fired a single round. We found a couple of them who were not dead, but seriously wounded. One of them could speak a little broken English, so we interrogated him. He was only sixteen years old, and scared to death. The other one died while this one was being interrogated. He told us that he was part of a work force, which was digging a tunnel. This is about all that we got out of him, before he died too. We radioed in our situation and were told to sit tight until the next morning. This may seem like a coward's way to fight a battle, but survival is the name of the game out here. Sometimes, you have to put your feelings to the side, and get the job done. I must admit, it sure was a lot different to kill someone like this, then to shoot the enemy in a firefight.

The next morning, our orders were to search the surrounding area. Only a short distance from this site, we located a rather large tunnel complex under construction. It was already an underground city. It had a very large, well-hidden entryway that led to four massive rooms. Intelligence later told us that these rooms would probably have been used for dispensary, kitchen, housing, and storage. Several squads could have stayed hidden down there, for several months if necessary. They figured that the main digging force was the ones that we took out the night before. There were lots of pots lying around in the rooms and outside the entryway. The surrounding stragglers that we kept running across must have been using these pots to dispense of the dirt from the hole. They were scattering it all over the countryside, so that it would not be detected. Some of this dirt was carried for miles away from the dig site. The project must have been going on for an awfully long time. A demolition team was brought in to blow up and destroy the tunnels and rooms. At least, maybe we delayed Charlie's plans for this project. We were airlifted out that afternoon, and returned to our base camp.

CHAPTER 17

GHOSTS OF BATTLES PAST

Payday only came around once per month for a soldier. It usually fell when we were out in the field on a recon mission, but this time was different. My unit was at the base camp on standdown, for several days and we were planning to unwind and have a little fun. We were not paid in the normal U.S. currency. We received our pay in MPC (Military Payment Certificates). They looked a lot like monopoly money and were about the same size. There were bills for all money denominations, both dollars and cents. Our U.S. currency was exchanged for MPC, when we first arrived in the country of Vietnam. A soldier could actually be court-marshaled, for having any U.S. currency in his possession. The military would exchange the MPC for Vietnamese money, so we could trade with the local store merchants. The Vietnamese people would gladly accept the MPC, so we usually used it, when we went to town. This wasn't officially allowed, but there was no way that it could be controlled. Periodically, the U.S. military would change the style and color of the MPC, currently in circulation, without any kind of a notice. They would set up times and locations for all the soldiers to exchange their old MPC for the new ones. The old bills became worthless at this time. The Vietnamese merchants could get caught holding some worthless money, unless they were able to get a soldier to make an exchange for them. It was illegal for this to be done, but some soldiers saw this as an opportunity to make some easy money. Some soldiers would charge the merchants a percentage for the exchange, and others would promise to make the exchange, but never returned the money to the poor store owners.

Some of the soldiers in Vietnam filled out an allotment form, which allowed the majority of their paycheck to be sent to someone back in the States. The combat soldiers who spent most of their time out in the field had no need for much money. There wasn't anything to spend it on out there and it was dangerous to carry a lot of cash around in your pockets. I only received $25 per month and the rest was sent home to my parents, who put it in a bank account for me. I was building up a nice little nest egg. I was planning to get married as soon as I got back home, so we would have a little money to get started with.

I didn't smoke or gamble, so my money was usually spent on items like toothpaste, soap, writing materials, and junk food. The PX at the Da Nang compound had a great selection of items, so I was going shopping after lunch. We got word of a USO show that would be at the enlisted men's club tonight, I would definitely be needing a little beer money for that. The show would consist of an Australian band and several dancing girls. We were all looking forward to seeing a female with round eyes. I always enjoyed the USO shows. They were usually oriental bands that tried to play American music and sang in English with a slight accent. At least, it would break the monotony of our boring lives. For some reason, all USO shows ended the same way. They would ask all the soldiers to join in and sing the famous sixties tune, "The Green-Green Grass of Home." We were all drunk and this would make us homesick, so we would leave the show crying. This usually led to several fights, before we got back to the barracks, but we still always looked forward to the next show.

The next few days were spent enjoying and entertaining ourselves. We made several trips into town and indulged in a lot of heavy drinking. This was our way of clearing our minds of those bloody and inhumane past missions and also the ones that were sure to come later. It was almost impossible to get a full night's sleep, because usually someone would wake up screaming and yelling from a flashback nightmare. Once this happened, it was real hard for any of us to fall asleep again. The excessive drinking seemed to help with this problem too.

The dreaded news of our next mission came as no surprise to us. We would be on a reconnaissance mission that would begin in the north-central region of the A-Shau Valley and take us westward, across the Laotian border and finally we would loop back into South Vietnam for the mission completion. We would be out in the bush between two and three weeks. Additional supplies would be dropped in to us by helicopter, as we needed them. It is impossible to carry enough rations, water, and ammo, for a mission of that length. We went to the supply room, to get everything that we would be needing, for the first few days. All of my fatigue uniforms were worn completely out, so I was issued some new ones. We had around sixteen hours, before we would be moving out. Our insertion would take place at first light, in the morning.

The underbrush was extremely thick and there was nowhere for the choppers to set down. We would have to repel into the area. As was our normal procedure, when we touched the ground, we took up battle positions and got in a small perimeter. As the choppers disappeared, we stayed in our positions for a few minutes to let our ears adjust to the surrounding sounds. We had a full recon squad of twenty-one this time. As we moved out in a line formation, I was placed in the slack-man slot. This was the second man in the patrol, directly behind the point man. We would be traveling southwest and the point man would set the pace, according to the terrain and his gut feelings. The first two days and nights passed by uneventful. We had not found any sign that warned us of recent enemy movements or activity in this region.

As we ate breakfast the third morning, Staff Sergeant Zumwalt shared some history about an area we would be entering today. We were facing a large tree covered hill and it was marked on our map as Hill 937. He told us that this hill was the site of the Battle of Hamburger Hill that had occurred almost exactly one year ago. He said the battle on this hill had raged on for ten to twelve days. The 101st Airborne Division had forty-six casualties and around four hundred men wounded during this engagement. They confirmed that about six hundred and thirty VC had been killed and they suspected that the numbers were a lot higher then that. A movie would be made about this battle in the eighties.

We started the incline up Hill 937 and it wasn't very long until we began to see definite signs of the past battle. Staff Sergeant Zumwalt had told us that the hill had been penetrated by over two hundred air strikes and continually bombarded by several artillery batteries. The further up the hill we climbed, the more damage we observed. Some of the trees had been blown completely out of the ground and others were dead from the charring and burning that was caused by the air strikes. There were numerous foxholes and trenches interlacing the hillside. We were warned to watch out for any un-detonated artillery rounds. We saw parts of destroyed weapons and equipment. I could visualize the battles and could see the death and destruction, all around me. The Americans had departed from the hillside a few days after all the battles had ended, and the VC moved back in and took control. I don't think that any VC would be hiding in the area now, because the Army had sprayed the area with Agent Orange to kill all the underbrush that could be used as camouflage. We would not be going all the way to the top of Hamburger Hill. We would be climbing about halfway up, then continue to the southwest. A chill ran over my body, as we continued through history. We proceeded around the center of the hill and started our decline, on the opposite side of where we had started this morning. My emotions were confused, because part of me wanted to get off of that hill as soon as possible, but the other side of me wanted to stay and defend Hill 937, for the soldiers who had given their lives to capture it from the VC. I kept glancing back over my shoulder, as sight of the hill became hidden by trees and underbrush. We set up a night bivouac and ambush site about one-half klick from the base of Hamburger Hill. The trees and foliage was not real dense in this area and we could see parts of Hill 937, as well as another hill that lay in our pathway ahead. We set up our ambush positions in the shape of a V. Our map showed a heavily used VC trail, not very far ahead of our positions, so we put out plenty of trip-flares and claymore mines. We went on full alert a couple of times during the night, because of unusual sounds in the distance, but nothing ever happened. One team member reported seeing some dim lights upon Hill 937, but out squad leader shrugged his shoulders and said that it was restless spirits of our fallen comrades. I don't know about the rest of the guys, but that didn't help my feelings very much. He told us that it wasn't unusual for the units in this area to hear voices and battle sounds from up on Hill #937 at night. The events of the prior night had made all of us extremely tense. It started misting rain around 0400 hours the next morning, and a fog bank began to move in.

It was still raining when the sun came up, so we knew that we were in for a miserable day. We had cold C-rations for breakfast, wiped our weapons down, and broke camp. Our positions in the squad formation had been reassigned, and that was fine with me. The VC trail came into view about mid morning. We checked it out and there was no doubt that it was used quite regularly and had probably been traveled during the recent night. This was probably where we kept hearing sounds coming from. Our squad leader received radio orders for us to set up an ambush on the east side and see what would wander into our trap. They wanted us to grab a couple POWs, but we would have to see how the cards fell. This exact spot had been used for an ambush before, because there was a shallow trench already dug, which ran parallel with the trail. The trench was just deep enough for a soldier to lay flat and be concealed by the brush in front of him. I'm not sure if the trench had been dug by Americans or the enemy. There was only one thing wrong with this situation. The trench was already filling up with rainwater, so we elected to drop back a few yards and settle down there. Charlie likes to move around in this kind of weather, so we were looking forward to a good day of hunting. It would have been hard to keep from falling asleep, except for the rain and insects. There were three very large anthills, not too far from where we were lying. Each one of these anthills must have been about four feet high, and bigger around than a man. Apparently, the rain had made some of the ants angry and they had swam over to take it out on us. Only a few made it to our positions, so we were able to withstand the assault. I was lying there watching them devour a poor grasshopper, which had just wandered into their kill zone.

It was late in the afternoon before we heard voices nearing our positions. There were five heavily armed NVA coming down the trail. They all seemed to be arguing and were in very bad moods. I don't think that we would have had a very good chance of talking these guys into surrendering. We opened fire on them and they tried to fight back, but they never even had a chance. We had the bodies in the brush and attempted to clean up any signs of the battle. We decided to stay in our same positions, throughout the night. We did place a few claymores around our positions for added comfort. We would spend the night at one-third alertness. This meant that we would have seven soldiers on guard at all times. The trail was only used once during the night. An elderly farmer came down the trail with a cart pulled by a water buffalo. The squad leader gave us a hand signal to let him pass.

As we prepared to move out the next morning, the rain had let up and the sun was trying to peep out, around the heavy clouds. We patrolled for about three hours and the point man signaled us to halt. We came across a South Vietnamese soldier. Sarge went forward to converse with the soldier. He could see an opening up ahead and there appeared to be a small village up there. These secluded villages were usually surrounded by booby traps, so we had to be extra careful as we entered the area. The point-man located two booby traps, almost immediately. One was a grenade that he replaced the pin in, and the other was a hidden pit of punji stakes. We entered the village and the residents were running around doing their daily chores. They didn't give us any resistance but things just didn't seem normal. We figured that some VC probably lived here, but if not, then they definitely used it as a rest stop when passing through this region. We were probably looking at some active VC activists right now. We fanned out and started to search the village. There were eight-ten hooches made out of clay and straw, and a covered storage shed that was used for rice and grain. Several pigs and a milk goat were standing around in the area. We attempted to interrogate the residents, but they would not give us any useful information. They denied any knowledge of VC activities in the surrounding areas. We continued our search and found a cache of weapons under a feed trough behind one of the hooches. It contained two AK-47 assault rifles, six SKS carbines, and a small selection of grenades and ammo. Of course, no one had any knowledge of it being there. We also found a tunnel entry under a pile of hay. The hole was empty, except for a very poisonous viper that had been placed in there. The hole was big enough for five or six soldiers to hide. None of the residents had ever seen this before either. A couple of the team members were getting upset and wanted to kill everybody in the village. There were no children or old people in the village, and that was extremely unusual. We radioed in our news and headquarters was very concerned about our findings. They were going to send us a couple of interpreters who were trained in enemy interrogation. There was a garden area that was big enough to set a chopper down. The chopper would drop them off, then immediately take off again. They were afraid that the VC in the surrounding area would converge on a downed chopper. We were to secure the village and guard the visitors. We were all shocked when the bird set down. Two South Vietnamese soldiers jumped out and one of them was a female. The chopper was back in the air, as soon as their feet hit the dirt. The male soldier spoke excellent English and started explaining everything to our sergeant. The female soldier started yelling at the villagers and was waving her pistol around and pointing it at them. I didn't know whether to take cover or laugh. One poor fellow must have answered her wrong, because she slapped him across the side of the head, with the side of her gun. He hit the ground and was out like a light. She kicked him a couple of times and then moved on to the next one. This went on for a while, and every so often, she would pull one out of the group and bind his hands with grass rope. After they were bound, they were separated from the rest. When the interrogation finally ended, she had bound four gooks: one female and three males. The chopper was called back in and her prisoners were loaded. As the bird was disappearing in the evening sky, we heard one gunshot and something fell from the chopper door. We all just looked at each other, and didn't say a word. We were ordered to torch the village and destroy all the food and supplies, before we moved out. I didn't like the idea of killing the innocent animals, but we had our orders. The orders could have been worse than that. We hit the trail and would be setting up for the night a short distance away.

The next three days and nights went by uneventfully. We did encounter a sniper on a path one day. He shot a hole through one team member's canteen. The guy got extremely mad, but was unharmed. A properly aimed M-79 grenade round brought the sniper and most of his tree down with him. The sniper fired one round and we fired one round. I'm not sure if this could be considered as a firefight.

We were beginning our second week in the field, and we should be nearing the Ho Chi Minh Trail and the border of Laos. Some unit was engaging in some heavy contact somewhere up ahead. We had been listening to it for about a half-hour and we were rapidly approaching the area. The radio informed us that a small unit of Marines were pinned down and couldn't move in any direction. They were holding their own, but couldn't last much longer. They were informed that we would be there shortly and clear the back door for them. We could then scrutinize the situation and determine our alternatives. The Marines had made a bad choice and had tried to cross a sparsely covered area and the gooks surrounded them from the wood lines. They must have known that they were coming and set up the trap. As we neared the battlefield, we formed a line formation and marched ahead. We were able to pick off several of the enemy, before they knew that we were there. The others tried to fight back, but were losing men, so they started retreating to the flanks of the Marines. The Marines kept adding to their misery. The Marines were able to back out to the wood line, and join forces with us. My squad had one wounded man. He had a real serious chest wound and would require an immediate medevac. He was in shock and was going in and out of consciousness. The medic was doing everything that he possibly could to make him hold on until help arrived.

The Marines had not been as fortunate. They had three dead soldiers and four others were wounded. Two were in serious condition. The medevacs were called in and we secured the area for their arrival. The Marines said that they had never been so happy to see a bunch of Army grunts. One of them wanted all of our addresses, so he could write us when we all got back to the States. The four choppers arrived within forty-five minutes. One of them was a gunship and it continued circling the area for air support. The others loaded their cargo and took off fast. We later got a radio report that our man had died, while in surgery. I knew him well and planned to write his family and let them know what a good soldier he was. The enemy had no way of knowing the size of our force, so they had departed the area, with their tails between their legs. A Chinook helicopter arrived shortly and transported the remainder of the Marine unit out. We exchanged our goodbyes and we hit the trail again. We had lost a good portion of the day at this spot, so we would not make it to the border today. It was a sad day for us, because of the loss of our buddy, but we had been able to save the rest of the Marines and we felt pretty good about that. We were real short on supplies, so we had them bring us some goodies, before dark. This was our second supply drop, since we had left on the mission.

The next few days, we kept ourselves busy with ambushes along the Ho Chi Minh Trail and the Laotian border. We kept moving around and had some surprises waiting on the VC in this area. We had gathered a nice number of kills, without any harm to our team members. The Sarge said that we were pushing our luck, and we needed to get out of this region. We crossed into Laos and started to sweep that region. This was my first time to enter Laos and I felt like I was breaking somebody's rules. I had been in Cambodia on several occasions and I had felt the same way then. I remember, in one of my letters from home, Dad had sent me a clipping out of our hometown newspaper. It said that the American troops were entering into Cambodia for the first time. I had already been in there twice and others had crossed that border before my group. Some of the news that the American public received about the Vietnam War, was a long way from being truthful.

One morning we broke camp and proceeded down a path. Only a short distance away, we walked straight into the middle of a recon unit's bivouac area. We surprised each other and a fierce firefight broke out. Our point man and slack man took hits and were out of the action. The gooks fought their way back into the woods and retreated. We killed four of them and blood trails told us that a couple of more had been seriously wounded. One of our men had been killed when he was struck in the head by a round. The other two had a leg wound and a shoulder wound. We would have to find a spot where a chopper could come and get them. We had to send them up through the trees, in mobile litter baskets. This would cut our manpower strength down to sixteen members. Our hearts were saddened once again. The kid killed was a brand-new father. I wondered if it should have been me, instead of this young man. We should be looped back to the Vietnam border by late tomorrow evening.

The night had been quiet and we were making good time today. We neared the Vietnam border in plenty of time to set up an effective night ambush. Our rations were almost expended, so we skipped supper. About 21:30 hours, we attacked a ten-man unit, moving down the Ho Chi Minh Trail. We had seven kills before the others were able to run away. We moved down the trail a short distance and set up a new ambush site. About 04:00 hours, we took out three VC on bicycles. We had taken no hits during these firefights. The next morning, we were notified by radio that we had to get out of that area, as quickly as possible. A reconnaissance plane had viewed several groups of VC, converging on our location. The gunshots from the night before must have alerted the VC to our presence and they were coming after us. They were almost on top of our position. We broke camp and started heading eastward, at a steady pace. We were only about three klicks from our assigned pickup point. Gunships were in route to aid us from the air, if they caught up with us. We were almost at a trot and we were beginning to feel pretty good. About two thirds of the way to our pickup point, a sniper started shooting at us and had us pinned down. We could not locate him in the tree line and was totally at his mercy. The enemy was on our heels, so we knew that decisions had to be made quickly. We would put lots of firepower out and hope to keep the sniper's head down. We would start to fan out in flanks until someone spotted the sniper. Believe it or not, it worked and one of our men saw the sniper sitting on the limb of a tree, and he shot him out of the tree. We grouped back up and took off again. The radio informed us that a chopper pilot was reporting that the VC were moving in on us, from about three hundred yards out. They probably had figured out our destination. Our equipment was slowing us down, but fear was making up for it. A Cobra helicopter began spraying the area to our rear, with mini-gun rounds. These little buggers spit out six thousand rounds per minute and surely that would slow some of them down. We could see the clearing of our pickup point, but enemy troops had two sides of the zone covered and the hueys would not be able to land. We took up battle positions in our tree line and engaged in an allout firefight to the end. We popped two red smoke grenades to warn the choppers of a hot zone. A chopper pilot did not have to pick up soldiers under a red smoke warning. Despite the warning and the known dangers, the hueys lined up and started coming in for our pickup. We had another casualty occur, while the first chopper was loading. The dead soldier was tossed on board and they took off. The next two birds were loaded without incident from our team members, but a door-gunner was seriously wounded. I was in the group that was left for the last chopper and things did not look real promising. We were beginning to receive fire from the rear, as well as the front. The gunships were doing their best, but there were a lot of trees for the enemy troops to hide behind. The last huey hit the ground and we set out running for it. The soldier in front of me went to the ground, with a bullet in his right thigh. I helped him hobble to the chopper and boosted him in. I dove through the door, just as the chopper started to lift off the ground. The rounds were peppering the sides of the chopper, as we began to gain altitude. Tears began to run down my cheeks, as I thanked God for bringing me safely through another mission.

CHAPTER 18

A REALLY BIG SNAKE

Over the past two months, our original recon team had dwindled down to only eight members. When I became part of this unit we had forty-four men. All of us never went out on a single mission together, but our rotation system allowed us to work occasionally with everyone and we had become a very tight group. Each one of us had over six months combat experience and we knew that we could depend on each other when the cards were down. We occasionally got a new recruit to replace someone leaving, but all of a sudden we were stuck with a lot of new and inexperienced soldiers.

This was real scary for us, because most of our missions required both experience and reliability, for the survival of the whole team. Our numbers had declined for several reasons. During the last two months, we had been on some really dangerous missions that had cost the lives of about a dozen good men and more than that had been seriously wounded and were sent back for medical attention. Of course, about ten of our guys had successfully completed their Vietnam tours and rotated back to the States, to exit the Army or be reassigned. I was near the end of my first tour, but I had already volunteered to come back for another hitch. Right now, I wasn't real sure that I had made a wise decision.

For once, the brass (officers who scheduled our missions) were using their heads. They were going to give us a couple of weeks to give these guys some training. Of course, they had all already been through the normal basic infantry training, but nothing to compare with what we would put them through. We hoped that they would even get to dodge a few enemy bullets, before we got them involved in any serious firefights. You never know how a person will react, when his life is threatened. We would be taking them out on several recon patrols, in the Qui Nhon area. This region was pretty quiet right now, but surely we would be able to stir up a couple of VC, for training purposes. We would be dividing the group up into four teams and I would be the squad leader for one of them. More than half of these guys had been in country less than a week. It was obvious because of their goofy questions and their brand-new jungle fatigues. They even had the toes of their jungle boots spit-shined. When I met with my squad the first time, I made them take some sand and dull the finish off the boots. I explained to them that a shiny boot could reflect light and be seen from a long distance. I took them out to a practice range and found out what kind of marksmen they were. We selected a man to be my M-60 machine gunner and even found one that was a fairly accurate shot with an M-79 grenade launcher. I spent the rest of the day helping them to get their combat equipment together, and explaining our mission goals to them. I kept mentioning to them about staying alive, because I wanted to get it through their heads that they were in a real war zone now. One of the original recon members was assigned to me and he would be our point man. His name was Corporal Bobby Mullins and he was from Georgia. We had survived several serious missions together and were pretty good friends.

Our first mission would be a simple one. We would simulate a routine recon patrol for three days and our objectives would be to teach them about reading enemy signs, avoiding and recognizing all types of booby traps, and the basics of setting up effective and safe perimeters. We would march right out the main gate of the Qui Nhon compound and the mission would begin. I hoped that we would not have any enemy contact on this phase of their training.

We exited the gate at 04:00 hours and Corporal Mullins took up his position at point. I was bringing up drag at this point, for observation purposes. The guys were nervous, but you could also feel their excitement. Both of these are good traits, for a combat recon member. We did some serious nonstop humping till around noontime. This was to build up their stamina and get them used to the heat and terrain. The temperature was near 110 degrees right now and would probably rise another eight to ten degrees today. Some of these guys were really hurting when I called for a halt, but I had heard very little complaining from any of them. They had a variety of sunburns and blistered feet. After they all collapsed onto the ground, I reminded them about the many types of poisonous snakes in this region. I spent the remainder of the day showing them how to set up different style perimeters, depending on the terrain and the objective of their mission. While this was going on, I had sent Corporal Mullins ahead to set up a variety of booby traps that we could encounter the next day. We had brought along some special supplies that he would need for this. Corporal Mullins returned late in the afternoon and gave me thumbs up. This was to let me know that the next training phase was in place. Since most of our missions involved night ambushes, we prepared one for the night. We only had a ten-man squad, so I formed a line perimeter along the edge of a streambed. We would be on fifty-percent alertness throughout the night. We used some C-4 and warmed some Crations for supper and settled down for the night. One guy said that he had heard something and popped a parachute flare during the night, but I am sure that it was just his imagination.

The second day was spent in a relatively small area. Our point man weaved through underbrush and down trails. He had plotted this course and had concealed all sorts of booby traps along the way. He would halt the patrol, prior to reaching one, then he would bring the group up to try and locate it. After they all had an opportunity to find it, then he would explain how it was constructed and activate it so they could see its destructive capabilities. Corporal Mullins had done an excellent job setting up the course. He had used a number of different type booby traps. He had hidden some buried punji stakes, rigged grenades without pins, and even had a poisonous arrow that would shoot across a pathway. He had them concealed so well that I even had trouble locating a couple of them. The trainees asked a number of questions and seemed to realize the danger of these little devices. We shared some true stories, about how these things had maimed and killed some of our buddies. We set up that night in a small circular ambush site.

We would spend day three patrolling some areas that would eventually wind us back to the Qui Nhon compound. We would take some trails that were regularly used by the local farmers and peasants. This would allow us the opportunity to teach them about footprints and other important trail signs. We would probably even pass a few gooks along the way. A recon squad relies a lot on hand signals when they are in an area that requires silence. We had been teaching these signals to the guys along the way. One of the paths took us through some dense underbrush along a streambed. The point man raised a clenched fist, signaling the squad to halt, and sent word for me to come forward. I figured that he had spotted some VC, so I quietly worked my way to where he was at. As I neared him, he pointed down the pathway ahead. I started to ask him what was so unusual about a log, and then I saw it move.

I turned to him and said, "Is that what I think it is?"

He said, "Yeah I believe that it is!" He signaled for the squad to move out and we crept toward the log. It was the biggest snake that I have ever seen in my life. We all just stood around and stared in amazement. One of our team members was from the Philippines and he said that they had some really big snakes over there, but he hadn't ever seen one nearly this big. Apparently, he wasn't afraid of it, because he jumped on its back and rode it like a horse. It wormed its way through the underbrush and entered an open area. We had some six-foot lengths of perimeter rope with us, so we decided to measure this monster. The Philippino was the only one brave enough to hold the rope on the end of the snake's nose. The length of the snake was twenty-one feet and six inches long. The center of it was as big as a man's torso. Corporal Mullins and I had heard stories about these snakes swallowing small babies in some of the villages. I know now that it was definitely a possibility. We decided that since we were in a safe fire zone that we would dispose of this menace. I always kept a small camera with me, so we took a few pictures, before we opened fire. We backed off and let him have it with everything we had, including the M-60 machine gun and the M-79 grenade launcher. We tore him up pretty good. There was a big knot in the middle of the snake. I took my K-bar knife and cut the area open. There was a partially digested baby deer inside him. This thing was a nuisance to society. Corporal Mullins said that he thought that it was probably a Burmese python. He stripped off a section of the snake's skin, so he could take it back and show everyone back at the camp. We finished out the day with no problems and made it back to camp safely. We all had a wild story to share with the other guys.

We would be staying in base camp for two days, and then I would take them out on another mission. This would give them a little time to rest up and clean their equipment. We would be entering a lot heavier terrain this time and we would be humping up the side of a small mountain. Corporal Mullins would be going back out with me again. We still did not expect any enemy contact. We would be focusing on endurance and more night ambushes. The mountain would allow us more observation, of the surrounding area. We would be inserted into the area by helicopter this time.

The choppers set down, a short distance from the base of the mountain. As we exited the choppers on the drop zone clearing, Corporal Mullins took point and we immediately entered a patch of elephant grass. The guys found out real quick, what this particular vegetation could do to your exposed skin. One poor fellow got his left forearm ripped open pretty deep. We had to stop and doctor his wound. He wanted to know if he would get a Purple Heart for this injury. I just laughed at him and said, "I don't think so, but I will try to get you in a firefight later today, if you really want one." I don't think he appreciated my sense of humor. We started the climb up the mountainside. The trees and underbrush were real thick, but the worst part was the thousands of tiny loose rocks that were hidden by the brush. These guys were doing a lot of huffing, puffing, and grunting. I told them that was the reason that we had been nicknamed grunts. We had been moving a couple of hours when a team member slipped and tore his knee open on a sharp rock. It required some first aid, so everyone got to take a short break. I told them that we were going to need a medevac, before we reached our destination. About two-thirds of the way up the mountain, we set up an arch perimeter, for our night ambush. I had managed to confiscate a starlight scope from the supply room, so we were able to observe the valley floor that night. There was nothing at all. We scaled to the top by mid afternoon, the next day. It was obvious that this place had been used as an observation point in the past. There were trenches dug and remains of an old campfire site, but it had not been used recently. We found a broken chopstick, so I figured that it must have been a VC camp area. We set up camp and I allowed the squad to relax that afternoon. I kept two of them on watch, at all times. That night, the starlight-scope allowed us to observe three VC traveling down one of the paths. I woke everyone up to see the enemy. We also saw a small American recon squad, on the valley floor. It may have been one of the other training groups, doing some night maneuvers. We could hear some artillery rounds exploding in the distance, but they were too far away for us to see. We broke camp at daybreak and headed back down the mountain. We reached our pickup point around 20:00 hours. We radioed for the choppers and they were there within minutes, to load us up. I had planned on taking these fellows back out for one more training mission, but the brass had other ideas. The enemy activity had picked up around Dac To and Kontum. We would be putting together a search and destroy recon team and head in that direction in a couple of days. The new mission would involve several of the guys in my training squad. I hoped that Corporal Mullins and I had managed to teach them a few things that might help to keep them alive. We were assured of heavy enemy contact on this next trip.

Chapter 19

SHORT-TIMER

Everyone in Vietnam had a short-timer's calendar. I can't remember where or when I got mine. It just sort of appeared on my bunk one day. The calendar was actually a sketched picture with lines dividing it into 365 sections. It looked liked a jigsaw puzzle, but the pieces did not come apart. Each section represented a day of your one-year tour in Vietnam. At the end of each completed day, you would color in one of the sections. The sections were numbered 1 through 365. If you started coloring in the number 365 first, you could glance at the calendar and always know how many days you had left in country. When a soldier got below 30 days, he was considered as a short-timer. The calendar pictures varied, but most of them had something to do with the anatomy of the female body. A soldier's short-timer's calendar was very special to him. It usually hung at the head of his bunk, and nobody else would mess with it.

The ones who went out on field missions especially enjoyed our calendars. Sometimes we would be out in the bush for two or three weeks, so when we got back to the base camp, we could color a big hunk of the calendar. This was a real attitude booster. Small things like this really made a big difference in our lives.

Fear was something that a combat soldier had to live with every day during his tour in Vietnam. There seemed to be different stages and different types of fear. A soldier who was new in country was scared of everything, especially the unknown. A soldier's first time in a firefight is full of unknowns. His biggest fear is how he will react when the enemy shoots at him for the first time. It doesn't matter how much training a person has been through, the reality of being shot at or killed, has to be dealt with individually. Most will react properly, but some may coward down and freeze. A battle must be fought with teamwork or nobody will survive. The weak have to be weeded out quickly. Other unknown fears are terrain, climate, fitting in with their assigned group, and the local people. Fears can usually be overcome, by time and experience. As a soldier becomes a hardened veteran, he faces some new kinds of fear. This is the fear of overconfidence, or not caring anymore. When a soldier becomes overconfident, sometimes he will realize it, and sometimes he doesn't. If he doesn't realize it, in a combat situation, he will be more careless and is not as aware of what's going on around him. This can be deadly for himself, as well as his fellow squad members. His superiors must recognize this and help him get control of the situation. When you get to the point of not caring what happens to you in combat, then it really is time for a mind adjustment. Your fear is that you will have to face the same terrible things again that you have already made it through once. You feel that ending your life would have to be better than continuing like it is going. This is a form of suicide, and suicide is the coward's way out of a bad situation. The worst part about this is that he will probably take some of his buddies with him.

The last kind of fear that a soldier faces is that of being a shorttimer. When his tour is almost over, he tends to become overcautious. Being overcautious can make a soldier do dumb things.

A good example of this would be; a soldier might spend too much time in one spot, looking for a nonexistent booby trap, and a sniper might have extra time to zero in on him. This fear could also be fatal for him, and possibly his comrades.

The last few days of a combat tour can make a soldier have many mixed emotions. He is sad because he is leaving some very special friends behind. The relationship that is formed by serving in combat with a person is one that cannot be explained. They have lived together in some of the most disgusting and unbearable conditions possible. They have laughed together and they have cried together. They have shared happy letters from home and they have shared the sorrow of death in their families. They have watched friends die and they have shared in the celebration of a friend completing his tour and going home. They have proven through their actions on the battlefield that they were willing to give their very lives, for their friends. This is what friendship is all about. They always promise to keep in touch, but they know that they will probably never see or hear from them again. I'm not sure, if it is tougher on the one staying behind, or the one going home. There is a deep sense of guilt that a soldier takes home with him, when he leaves his buddies behind in a war zone.

A solider will never be able to answer the question, "Why did I make it home alive, when so many of my friends did not?" This is a pain that he will have to live with until his dying day.

CHAPTER 20
AN KHE PASS

I had been assigned to a small security group in Long My, Vietnam. Our duties included the security of a large ammunition storage facility and its surrounding compound. We were to accomplish this task, by utilizing two APCs (Armored Personnel Carriers). This ought to be real interesting, because I was the ranking NCO of this group, and I didn't know one thing about an APC. I had seen them used in combat situations, especially down in the Mekong Delta region, but I had never even rode on one. I filled out some forms and they issued me a military driver's license that showed an unlimited vehicle weight.

I was introduced to my squad and they took me out to see the new toys that I was in charge of. An APC is a big ugly armored box. It was rectangular in shape and only came in the color of olive drab green, which was the same color as the underwear that I had on. It moved on a set of tracks that allowed it to go almost anywhere. The rear was a giant hydraulically controlled door that let down and formed a ramp. The inside of these things were really unique. There was a small compartment in the left front section that was where the driver sat. The area was very small and tight, so the size of the driver was limited. The seat sort of resembled one off of an old John Deere tractor. The seat would rise up or down, to allow the driver the option of having his head inside the vehicle or outside the vehicle, when it was in operation. There was an armored hatch door above the driver that could be sealed and locked from the inside. If his hatch was closed and his seat was down, he could still drive the vehicle, by viewing his surroundings through periscope type windows. The steering was controlled by sticks. Behind the driver was an open compartment area that was the entire width of the APC. There were areas for storage and each side had a bench styled seat that would swing down, to allow a place for soldiers to sit. There was a turret area in the right front portion of this open compartment. It had a seat similar to the driver's, and also had a hatch door above it. The person seated here, could raise himself up and have access to an M-60 machine gun. There was a large door in the center roof that could be opened, also. There was a giant search light on top of the APC, to view the surrounding area. The APC was equipped with a 50-caliber machine gun and a spot to mount the M-60 on top. Some of these vehicles were diesel powered, but both of ours had gasoline powered engines in them. The mechanic said that one had a 289 cubic inch Ford engine and the other had a 327 cubic inch Chevrolet engine. I don't have a clue, because all engines look alike to me. They would run between forty-five and sixty miles per hour, depending on the load and the terrain. The most amazing thing about the APC was that it would float. We could cross rivers and not have to worry about the depth of the water. The entire thing would be under water, except maybe the top twelve inches. Even though it was airtight when totally sealed up, it came equipped with bilge pumps, in the event of a leak. We would drive it out in the middle of a river and use it for a raft while we went swimming. After the gates of the compound were secured at night, we were the only ones who were allowed to go outside the perimeter. During the day, we usually rode around the areas that surrounded our compound. We would check out the farmers and local peasants who were in the area. We became familiar with them and even knew a lot by their name. At night we stayed closer to the perimeter fences, but sometimes we would slip down into the little town of Long My. This was not real smart of us, because I am quite sure that some VC must have lived in the village. The main purpose and objective of our security role, was to deter any enemy infiltration, by our unscheduled patrolling presence and tremendous firepower. We were successful most of the time. We got into an occasional skirmish, but most of them were minor.

Another one of our duties was to provide convoy escort between Quin Nhon and Pleiku. This was not an everyday role, but sometimes we were used for backup security. Occasionally, one of us would go along as a gunner on the back of a jeep, but usually we took one of the APCs. The jeeps would have a tripod mounted in the center of the jeep floor, and dual M-60 machine guns were mounted on top of it. The gunner stood behind these guns and could turn them in any direction that was needed. We normally didn't get any enemy activity on a day escort, but the nights were rather hectic. It was unusual to make a complete night run, without at least a few harassment rounds fired from a sniper, somewhere along the route.

There was only one way to make this trip, and that was straight up highway QL-19. This took us straight through the dreaded An Khe Pass. The town of An Khe was halfway between Quin Nhon and Pleiku. The road took us up some steep winding mountainous roads. The pass was a little east of town. This was one of the steepest grades of the trip and the heavy laden trucks would have to gear down and creep up the side of the mountain. This would make the convoy very vulnerable to an ambush. The top of the pass was known as the Hairpin. There were several destroyed military vehicles along this area, to remind us of past convoy demises. Most of the roadside had very little underbrush, because it was continually being sprayed with Agent Orange.

It was around 5:30 a.m. when we started the steep climb up An Khe Pass. I had volunteered to ride gunner on one of the jeeps tonight. It was a beautiful night and I was looking forward to the adventure. Some people are too dumb to learn that you should never volunteer for anything, especially in the military. We had reached an area that had a cliff on the right side and a pretty good drop off, on the left side. The convoys usually ran right down the middle of the highway, because we were the only ones on the road. About that time, the lead vehicle ran over a land mine and exploded into flames. The hill on our right became alive with automatic weapons fire, down the entire length of the convoy. Mortar rounds and RPGs began coming in and hitting the vehicles. A mortar round hit under the front of our jeep and it threw me out the back. I crawled around and found my M-16, which had been lying at my feet in the jeep. I headed for the left side of the road and slid over the edge. I half stumbled and fell for about twenty feet. I knew that we had to get away from the vehicles, before they all blew up. Some of them were loaded with high explosives and ammunition. I saw and heard other soldiers sliding down the roadside. The gooks had picked a perfect spot for the ambush, but they hadn't considered how vulnerable their positions would be, once the explosions began. We were below the road level and only had to worry about falling objects. They had to be concerned about being a target when the ammunition started to ignite. We had all taken refuge behind large rocks. The enemy silhouettes would be visible against the skyline, if they tried to come over the roadside after us. We should be able to pick them off, one by one. One of our men had grabbed a radio out of a truck and had radioed our situation and location. Help would be on the way at first light, and that was only about thirty minutes away. It would take the gooks a long time to flank our position and we felt pretty confident that we would be able to hold on till the choppers arrived. Besides, it sounded like the gooks were rather busy right now, dodging the exploding rounds. It sounded like a shooting gallery up there.

As dawn broke, we could hear the whipping sound of choppers approaching our location. Apparently, the gooks who had not been seriously wounded or killed had retreated the area. Several American soldiers lost their lives on that dreadful morning, and lots of vehicles and supplies were destroyed, but it could have been a total disaster. This was just one more story to be told, about the famous An Khe Pass.

CHAPTER 21

INCOMING

I was up and stirring, well before the sun came up. It had been one of those miserable, restless nights that we become so used to in Vietnam. A combination of nightmares and the unbearable heat, had kept me from getting much sleep. We had come into our base camp on the prior day, from eighteen days in the field. We were promised three days to rest, but we really didn't expect it. The Viet Cong were extremely active right now, and we could be sent out again at any moment.

Some of the other guys were still asleep, so I tried to stay as quiet as possible. I sat on my foot locker and tried to gather my thoughts, about the events that had taken place, over the last two and a half weeks. The last mission had really seemed to take a toll on me, mentally and physically. One of my closest friends had been killed, and two other soldiers in my squad had been wounded. The mission had taken us through some of the roughest terrain of the Central Highlands region. Our intelligence information was totally inaccurate and even our maps had some flaws. We knew that we would make enemy contact, but we were told to only expect light resistance of a squad size Viet Cong force. This held true for the first two weeks. Everything seemed to be going as planned. Then one evening, we encountered a company size regiment of North Vietnamese regulars. If it had not been for our great air support, none of us would have made it out alive.

After breakfast, I returned to the hooch and sat down to plan out the events of my day. I planned to get all of my chores done today and hoped to spend tomorrow resting up. It would take the majority of the day to clean my clothes and equipment. A soldier's gear can get in pretty bad shape, when he is in the field for an extended period of time. His weapon is cleaned and maintained as often as possible, but his other gear has to wait.

By noontime, I had finished washing my clothes, and made a pretty good dent in getting my gear back in shape. I went to the chow hall to eat lunch and it was great. I can't remember what we had, but I know that it was great. It was warm, and not out of a can. When you have been out in the field, eating cold C-rations for several days; then you get the opportunity to enter a building, sit down and eat a hot meal of any kind, it tastes wonderful. The guys who never leave their compound are always fussing about the food, but they should have to try our side of the war for a change. It would make them appreciate a real egg, or a glass of iced tea.

After finishing lunch, I went back to the hooch and continued cleaning and preparing my gear. We had several new guys in our squad who always wanted to wait on getting their combat gear ready, until the last minute. I felt that my life could depend on this equipment, so I tried to keep it maintained and ready, at all times. I still had a little M-16 ammo left from the last mission, so I decided to wait until we received our next orders, before I would draw additional ammo, grenades, flares, and claymore mines. The type of weaponry that we carried usually was dependant upon the mission. We certainly didn't want to carry anything that we would not be needing. We also wanted to make sure that we had everything for any situation that may occur. The equipment and weapons that a soldier carries, is dependent upon his job or the position that he fills in a combat squad. I normally go on a mission with a recon squad of thirteen to twenty-one men. Our weapons usually consisted of one 12-Ga. shotgun, two M-60 machine guns, one M-79 grenade launcher, one or two 45 Cal. pistols, and the rest would normally have M-16 rifles. Some of us might even carry a Russian or Chinese AK-47 instead of our M-16. We also had an assortment of grenades, mines, flares, and knives.

Finally, I felt that my gear was ready and I could move out, with a moment's notice. It was now mid afternoon and too hot to do much of anything, so I decided that I would try to catch up on some much needed letter writing. I was very loyal to write letters to my girlfriend and parents, even though sometimes they were back-dated, without their knowledge. After I got home, I remember hearing my girlfriend say that she would sometimes go several days without receiving a letter, and then suddenly a bunch would come in. Nobody else received a letter from me regularly. I would try to write when I was in the field, but sometimes it just wasn't possible. I never let my folks or girl know about my missions. I would always talk about the daily routines around the base camp. I would sometimes write two or three letters in the same day and date them different. This would help me to cover up for the times that I spent in the field. I think that I remember writing seven letters that day.

Along about dusk, I decided to lie down and take a short nap. The other guys in the hooch were making too much noise for me to really rest, but I figured that I could at least close my eyes for a while and pretend. I had only been lying there about thirty minutes, when all hell broke loose. It sounded like the entire compound was being blown to bits. We were receiving mortar rounds and intense small arms fire from somewhere outside the perimeter. It sounded like it was coming from all sides. We needed to get to the safety of our bunkers, but were scared to go in any direction. We knew that the enemy would try to pinpoint hits on all the buildings, so we had to make a move quickly. I don't know if I was more frightened or the dumbest, because I was the first one to grab my weapon and ammo and run out the door. It seemed like the whole world was on fire and continuing to blow up. I zigzagged and dodged explosions until I finally made it into the safety of the closest bunker. Several other soldiers had already beaten me in there. I then realized that I had very little ammunition to defend myself with. I would have to pick and choose my shots, and not waste any. The biggest problem was that we could not see where any of the enemy were at. They were well camouflaged and hidden. We would have to locate them by their muzzle flashes.

The barrage of incoming rounds continued heavily for more than ninety minutes. Then it began to slow down to an occasional mortar or rocket, with small arms harassment fire mixed in the middle. It was still enough to keep us pinned down and under their control. We knew that it would not do any good to send troops outside the perimeter, before daylight. They would pinpoint us and pick us off, one by one. They would also stay ahead of us and disappear into the night. We stayed in our positions and took turns on guard duty, throughout the night. If we thought that we saw movement, near our perimeter, we would pop off a couple of shots. The enemy knew that when it got daylight, the planes and helicopters would be in the air, and we would be coming after them. I'm sure that they departed the area, well before the sun came up.

As the sun arose, we began to come out of the safety of our bunkers and to access the damage that was entailed. The damage was extensive and their attack had been very successful. I never heard the exact number, but several American soldiers lost their lives and many more were wounded. My squad was sent out within a couple of hours, to recon the perimeter and surrounding area. We found a lot of signs, where the enemy had been, but no bodies or blood trails.

Most of the base camps and compounds in South Vietnam received these kinds of attacks regularly. They were not always as severe or successful as this particular one. The purpose was sometimes more for harassment to lower our morale than for destruction and death. If a sniper can kill one soldier, then the morale of the entire camp will be affected. All the camps and compounds had units that continually did recons around the outer perimeter, and many types of detection devices were used, but somehow the Viet Cong always managed to slip through and set up these attacks. Many good soldiers lost their lives while lying in their bunks, taking a shower, eating chow, or even writing a letter to his loved ones. I had heard some people say that there were places in Vietnam that were safe. As a combat veteran with two tours, I totally disagree with that opinion. I covered a lot of South Vietnam during my tours, and I never found "That SoCalled Safe Spot."

CHAPTER 22

SECRET MISSION

Everyone at the base camp was talking about a secret mission, which was coming up soon. Nobody seemed to know any details about it, not even how the rumor had got started. Guys were making up wild stories and the whole thing was getting blown out of proportion. The officers would not even confirm that such a mission was in the making. They said that we would find out soon enough, if something really was going down. After a few days, the rumors began to die down and everyone stopped talking about it.

About two weeks later, we were informed that they were looking for some volunteers, to be used in a SOG (Special Operations Group) mission. The task force would be made up of personnel from the Airborne Rangers, Army Special Forces, Marine Force Recon, and even a couple of guys from the Navy Seals. The rumors started again, because this really sounded like something big was about to take place. Initially, all we were told was that the mission would be extremely dangerous and there would not be any air support or standby ground troops available in the area. If the mission went sour, the task force would be on its own. This immediately told us that the mission would be taking place, in an area that American troops were not authorized to be sent into. This explained why they had started out, by asking for people to volunteer.

I was well into my second tour by now, so everyone already knew that I wasn't very smart. I turned my name in and said that I wanted to be a part of the task force. I was told that all volunteers would be interviewed individually and the chosen ones would be notified within a couple of weeks. They still had not shared any more details with us about the mission. There wasn't anything to do but wait. I continued to go out with my recon team, on two or three day patrols, for the next two weeks.

Finally, word came down from headquarters that a list of names would be posted on the bulletin board, the following morning. I didn't get much sleep that night, because I wasn't sure that I had made a rational decision. The next morning I was up early, but the list had not been posted yet. I went to breakfast and come back by to check again. Sure enough, there was my name on the list. The list consisted of about eighty-five men and I only recognized the names of about eight of them. All members of the task force would be transported to a secluded part of another base camp, about thirty miles away. We were told to bring our weapons and all of our combat field gear. We would receive other items, and ammunition, when we arrived.

Upon arriving at the compound, we were given very few details, and they broke us up into our assigned squads. We were only issued enough food rations, to last us for six meals. They told us that we would have to consume them sparingly. Luckily we would be having a good breakfast the next morning, before our scheduled flight out, at 05:00 hours. We had still not been given very many details. This had been listed as a need-to-know mission. We were given instructions that only applied to the portion of the mission that our squad would be directly involved. They also explained our E&E (Escape and

Evasion) orders, in the event that things did not go as planned. We were assigned an E&E partner, but if he was killed or got misplaced, then we would have to try and make it out by ourselves. We were to receive our final orders, when we reached our final drop-off point.

As we boarded the choppers, reality turned into fear and the unknown obstacles that were waiting for each of us. This group was made up of some seriously hardened veterans and I really felt out of place with them. The choppers took to the air and it was obvious that we were headed to the north. This meant that we were either headed into North Vietnam or part of northern Cambodia. Neither one was a very good option.

When the last chopper unloaded and had departed, you could have heard a pin drop. We divided up into our separate squads and received our final briefings. All of our gear was taped down, for a totally silent mission. We were told that there would be absolutely no spoken communication once we were given the order to go on silent mode. All orders would be given by hand signals. We were instructed to use heavy camouflage paint on all our exposed body parts. We were finally told what this mission was all about. We were going to cross the border and enter a POW (Prisoner of War) camp. We were to take whatever measures were necessary to bring back safely any American prisoners. This was all that we needed to hear at this point. We were gung ho to get started.

The trip to the camp would take a full two days. Once we were in striking range of the camp, my squad had the assignment of ensuring that one side of the camp was secure. We were told to stop anyone from entering or leaving the compound area. I would never actually get to see the inside of the POW camp. We were all excited to be a part of a rescue attempt, and we took this mission very seriously. We had no idea, what we would find at the camp, or what type of resistance might be waiting for us. We didn't know the physical shape of the prisoners or how well they would be able to travel. Some of them may not even be able to walk, so we had brought several stretchers along.

It was very dangerous to move a unit of this size, through enemy territory, without being seen or heard. All of our training techniques were being tested to the limit. We had to be aware of everything around us. I began to remember some things that I had been taught, back in basic training that did not seem to be important back then. Our squads rotated turns at walking point. We changed out regularly, to make sure that our senses did not let us down. We could not afford to make any mistakes, because it could jeopardize the entire mission, or possibly cost the lives of every member of this task force. The first day was uneventful and no enemy contact was made. There were a lot of signs, which showed recent presence of large groups of enemy troops, but they either stayed hid or had moved out earlier. We ate cold C-rations and settled down in our defensive positions, around the night perimeter. We had the guard duty divided up, so each soldier would get three hours of sleep. The skyline began to darken and the night creatures began to scurry around. It's always a good sign when the animals are moving around, but it can also make your imagination run wild. The night crept by slowly, but nothing happened.

We started out at daybreak the next morning. Our pace was set, so that we would not be arriving at the POW compound until it was early night. The camp would be invaded well after everyone had bedded down. We were getting close now and our nerves were on edge. At this point, I think that most of the fear was gone and anxiety of rescuing the American prisoners was all that we were thinking about.

We crept into our positions and set up the defensive perimeter around our side of the compound. The night was still and silent.

The invasion group was now beginning to enter the camp. We could not hear any of their movements, but we could feel them. It seemed like time had come to a halt, as we lay there waiting for the sounds of the evasion. It was inevitable that a battle would take place. We were prepared to fight back any incoming support from nearby. We didn't really know what to expect, but I think everyone was willing to give their lives for the cause. The silence continued and I began to wonder what was going on in there. It could mean that something good or bad, was taking place. News was finally passed around the perimeter that the mission was a failure and there were no POWs in the camp. It looked like everyone had hurriedly left the compound, maybe less than a day prior to our arrival. Our hearts were saddened and we all had a lot of questions. The main ones were: how did the NVA know about this mission and who told them when we would be coming? We still had to get back across the border, without being detected. This seemed impossible, since the enemy apparently knew that we were here. Our initial escape and evasion orders were to split up into two-man teams, but it was decided that we would be safer to go back out as a complete task force, just like we came in. We would put up one heck of a fight if anyone got in our way. We were to hold our present positions and start back at first light. Since our invasion had been known by the enemy, we figured that they would have ambushes and booby traps, to welcome us on the return trip across the border.

We stayed on full alert the rest of the night and no one got any sleep. We were all on edge and expected the worst. As first light began to break, we slowly moved out into our assigned positions. My squad was told to move out last. This was called closing the back door. At least we would not have to worry about the booby traps. As we rotated squad positions during the day, we were told that fresh tracks showed that additional enemy movement had taken place since we had come through the prior day. This made us even more uneasy and we could not understand why enemy contact had not been made.

As the day had drawn to a close, we had no choice but to stop for the night. It was much too risky to try and move during the dark hours. We set up our defensive perimeter and settled in for another extremely long night. We were all exhausted, so we worked out a sleep rotation system. Somehow, we made it through another uneventful night. I don't think that I had got any sleep that night either.

Daylight brought another long, dangerous day of unknown happenings. If we could keep up our normal pace and didn't make contact with Charlie, we should reach the border before the sun went down. We were still under silent movement orders, so we couldn't radio for pickup choppers, until we were back across the border. That might mean having to spend another night in the bush. None of us wanted that, but right now that was the least of our worries. I think we all said a silent prayer, as we moved out that morning. The point men continued to find heavy enemy sign, but no contact was made. It was, as if we were being watched by ghosts. We were all totally confused as we pushed onward. I was dead tired but my adrenaline and fear kept me going. Late that afternoon, we came to the border and safely crossed over. We radioed for the choppers, but were informed that we could not be picked up until the next morning. None of us had any rations left, so we settled down for a hungry night. For some reason, we felt safer on this side of the border, and some of us were able to get a little sleep. We were picked up the next morning and somehow, we had all survived another dangerous mission. Not one shot was fired and to this day, I don't understand why the enemy allowed our departure and did not take advantage of attacking our task force.

CHAPTER 23

FREEDOM BIRD

I had been out on an extended mission and my normal Vietnam departure date had come and gone. When they finally issued me some new orders, I only had two days left in country. The out-processing procedures were sort of lengthy and I would have a hard time getting everything finished by then. I had to turn in my weapon and all my combat gear, right there at the base camp. I would then have to catch an air-hop to Cam Ranh Bay, to complete all the required paperwork, prior to catching the "Freedom Bird" back to the States. I had a brand-new SKS rifle that I had confiscated out of a cache on my last mission and I wanted to take it home, as a war memento. It was a semiautomatic weapon, so it was legal to ship home, but the paperwork that was required for such a thing usually took several weeks to get processed. I didn't have several weeks, so I was hoping to bypass the red tape and take it with me. I was hoping to give somebody a sob story and maybe they would bend the rules. I only had a couple of hours to say goodbye to my buddies. Several of them had experienced some really hairy missions with me. We shared some quick laughs about good times and we shared some tears about mutual friends who had been killed. We all promised to stay in touch and meet sometime later, back in the States. Three of my closest friends went with me to my chopper, to see me off. I sat in the doorway and waved goodbye, as the camp disappeared in the distance. All of a sudden, I realized that I did not have a weapon and I felt very vulnerable. I eased back out of the doorway and allowed my mind to wander.

I arrived in Cam Rahn Bay and caught a ride to the departure office, to begin my final paperwork. Everything seemed to be in order, but it would take several hours of the old "hurry up and wait" procedures. I tried talking to several people, but I was bluntly informed that my SKS rifle would not be leaving the country with me. During my hours of waiting, I mingled with a group of guys who had just arrived in Vietnam and were awaiting their first duty assignments. They were full of questions and treated me like I was some kind of hero or something. I felt sorry for these guys but I sure was enjoying the attention. One of the soldiers noticed my rifle and started to question me about it. I explained to him that I had got it while out on a search and destroy recon patrol and they wouldn't let me take it home with me. I explained to him that paperwork could be properly filed and it could be sent home. I was in the process of giving it to him, when the dummy offered me three hundred and eighty-five dollars for it. That was a lot of money in 1971. He didn't have enough sense to realize that in a few days he would probably be up to his elbows in them. I felt bad about taking his money, but I got over it pretty quick. My name showed up on the roster, for the next plane leaving the country. It would be taking off in six hours. We would be flying on a commercial plane back to the States.

My last couple of days in Vietnam had been filled with mixed emotions. I was looking forward to going back to the States, but I was also scared of the changes that had taken place. We had heard all kinds of news reports, about how the American people hated Vietnam Veterans. They were calling us baby killers, dopeheads, rapists, and murderers. I wasn't sure how I would react to these attitudes, because I felt like I had done my duty and served my country well. I had volunteered to go in the Army, and also had volunteered for both combat tours in Vietnam. Nobody owed me anything and I didn't expect a parade or any kind of recognition, but I did hope for a little bit of respect and appreciation for what I had been through.

My main concern was going back home to my family and friends. I knew that I had changed a lot and I wasn't sure if they could accept these changes. I had gone home six months ago for a thirty-day leave, but I tried to hide all my problems from everybody. The last three years of military life had matured me in many ways, but the last nineteen months of war had totally changed my identity. I may still look the same, but I was not still the naïve kid who had joined the Army at age seventeen. My morals had declined drastically and my outlook on human life was totally different. I had been trained and programmed to do whatever it took to survive, and that was scary. I had seen and done some really horrible things that most people could not even realize. I knew that I would have to live with these memories for the remainder of my life. I would not be going home as a hero, but only a survivor. I would forever remember seeing the faces of my fallen friends and always wonder, "Why was it them, instead of me?" or "Was there something more that I could have done to save them?" I would always think about children and families who had to go on without their fathers and loved ones, because I had caused their death. I will always wonder how God chooses the ones who survive combat missions. I think that I will always have a deep quilt, for being one of the survivors. My future life must have a purpose, so I have to keep searching for that goal.

As we walked out onto the tarmac to board our Freedom Bird, we had to walk between rows of stacked coffins that were all draped over the top with an American flag. They were filled with the bodies of soldiers who had been killed in the war. They were waiting to be loaded on a military transport plane that would take them on their last ride, back to the States and their grieving families. As we passed through the coffins, you could have heard a pin drop. Some of us were shedding tears, as memories flashed through our minds. Everyone remained solemn and climbed the stairs to our plane. We took our seats and received instructions from the beautiful Oriental stewardesses. I don't think that there was a dry eye in the group. Everyone was staring blankly out the windows and having mental flashbacks, from the past months. Some of the guys had not experienced any actual combat, but there was still a special bond between all of us. As the big bird taxied down the runway and finally lifted off the ground, the plane exploded with yells and cheers of freedom. It began to sink in that we were really headed home. We started chattering among ourselves and settled down for the long flight back to the States. We would be stopping over at Guam and Honolulu, prior to our arrival at Fort Lewis, Washington. The total time of the flights would be about twenty-six hours. We had plenty of time to exchange stories about our tours of duty, but most of the talk was about our families, homes, future plans, and especially our girlfriends.

I don't know how to express my feelings when the airplane tires touched down in Washington. Some of the guys actually kissed the ground when we exited the aircraft. We were kept away from everyone else and bused to the special facilities for Vietnam veteran returnees. We were told that we would be spending several days here, for all kinds of re-orientation classes. I wasn't sure what that word meant, but I knew that I was ready to go home right then. We had hoped to be heading straight home, but we should have known that the Army would have other plans. We would have to take an extensive physical examination, to make sure that we had not brought back some dreadful disease that might harm the innocent American people. The ones of us, who had been involved in actually combat, had to be analyzed by some psychiatrists, to determine if we were safe to turn loose in public. I felt like an animal that had rabies. Some of the group had completed the military time of service and others of us would be receiving our next duty assignments, so the out-processing procedures were different for all of us. As is normal with the military, most of our time was spent waiting for our names to be called. We had to be fitted for new "Class A" uniforms and given our unit citations, ribbons, medals, and patches. The uniforms had to be tailored and the necessary insignias sewn on, so this would kill a whole day. They showed us films of protests and riots, which had taken place over the last few years. This was to prepare us for the poor attitudes, of some ignorant and stupid Americans. They knew that some of us had short fuses and wanted us to try and avoid any confrontations. Supposedly, some "Green Beret" who was returning from Vietnam had got into a fight with three civilians at the airport. He had killed all three of them, when they started making fun of him and spit in his face. The local police had shot and killed the soldier, while trying to apprehend him. That would be a terrible way to end a military career. He had put his tail on the line for his country and his life had ended, because of some cowardly idiots.

I finally completed my out-processing and received my new orders. I would be going to be reassigned to the 82nd Airborne Division, Military Police Unit, at Fort Bragg, North Carolina. I had a thirty-day leave, before I had to report there. The military issued me a plane ticket home and I grabbed my bags and caught a shuttle to the airport. I must admit that I looked pretty sharp in my dress uniform, with all my decorations and sergeant stripes. I couldn't wait to see what my girlfriend would think of the new me. We were to be married in just a few days. I had already called about my arrival,

145

so my family and girlfriend would meet me at the New Orleans International Airport.

The trip home went by fairly well. I heard a couple of smirks and rude remarks, but for once in my life, I kept my cool and tried to stay out of any trouble. I spent my travel time eating junk food and drinking ice-cold soda pops. When we landed in New Orleans, my heart was about to pound out of my chest. When I entered the lobby at New Orleans, they were all waiting for me. I think they had arrived several hours early. Dad said that he did not want to take a chance on being late. I was saddened when I saw my mom and dad, because they looked like they had aged forty years. The pressure of my two tours had taken a real toll on them, especially my mom. She almost broke my back when she hugged me. My girlfriend had always been a sharp looking girl, but all of a sudden, she was the most beautiful woman in the world. I loved her so much and I didn't want to ever be away from her again. My brother and his wife were there also and they handed me my brand-new niece. I was scared to death to hold her, but I managed somehow. It had turned out to be one of the happiest days of my life. We had a two-hour car trip home, but it passed by quickly. They asked me very few questions about Vietnam, but I sure had plenty of questions for all of them. My mother said that she was going to fatten me up while I was at home.

GLOSSARY

AGENT ORANGE – An orange, colored dust chemical that was dispensed from the air, to kill foliage on the ground, that the enemy troops used for concealment.

A.I.T. – Specialty training in a particular job field. Usually takes place immediately after basic training was completed.

AIRBORNE – The title given to military personnel who are trained and qualified paratroopers.

AK-47 – Soviet made combat assault rifle. Capable of being fired semi-automatic or fully automatic. Used by mostly NVA soldiers, but was also popular among some specialized Americans forces. Fired a 7.62mm round and could produce 600 rounds per minute.

AO – Term used by the military for the "area of operations."

APC – Armored Personnel Carrier. It was an armored vehicle used for the transport of personnel or supplies. It was usually heavily armed and operated on tracks.

ARVN – Regular Army of North Vietnam.

A-TEAM – Name given to a U.S. Special Forces recon team. Usually consisted of about ten members. Used in many undocumented missions during the Vietnam War.

B-52 – Extremely large Air Force plane, used mostly for highaltitude bombing missions.

BASE CAMP – Area where field units could rest and resupply. Sometimes was the location of a division's headquarters. These areas were usually well fortified with concertina wire, bunkers, and guard towers.

BATTERY – Name given to a company size artillery unit. Their weapons were the big guns, known as howitzers.

BIRD – Any type of aircraft.

BIVOUAC AREA – An area that troops used for overnight stays or a temporary rest area.

BLOOD TRAIL – A trail of blood left by a wounded soldier, trying to escape the scene of a battle.

BODY BAG – A plastic bag used to transport a dead soldier from the field.

BODY COUNT – This was the real or estimated number of enemy soldiers, which had been killed, wounded, or captured during a mission.

BUSH – The term that an infantryman uses for the field.

C-4 – This was a plastic explosive used by the military, for destroying tunnels, bunkers, and supplies of the enemy. A small hunk of it could also be lit and used for heating C-rations.

C-7 – A small cargo plane, also known as the Caribou.

CACHE – An area where enemy supplies and weapons were hidden.

CHARLIE – Slang term for the NVA or Viet Cong soldiers.

CHINOOK – A large helicopter with two sets of blades. It was used for hauling cargo, or troops. Some were even equipped as mobile hospitals. Also known as CH-47.

CHOPPER – Slang name for a helicopter.

CLAYMORE – A type of anti-personnel mine that was placed above the ground. Its detonation would propel steel pellets up to 100 meters. It was used very effectively in perimeter situations.

COBRA – An assault helicopter that was armed with rockets, machine guns, and sometimes mini-guns. Very effective in support of ground troops. Also known as AH-1G.

COMPOUND – A military installation.

CONCERTINA WIRE – Accordion style barbed wire with razor-sharp barbs.

CONTACT – When gunshots are exchanged with enemy soldiers.

C-RATIONS – Canned meals used by field units. Eaten cold or hot.

DEUCE AND A HALF – Two-and-a-half-ton military truck used to transport troops or supplies.

DINKS – A slang word that the American soldiers used for enemy troops.

FATIGUES – The standard issued combat uniform.

FIREFIGHT – Exchange of gunfire with the enemy.

FLARE – Hand fired into air, to illuminate surrounding area. Descent was controlled by a small, slow floating parachute.

FRAG – Fragmentation grenade used to maim or kill the enemy.

FREEDOM BIRD – This was the aircraft that was used to transport American soldiers from Vietnam back to the States.

GOOK – Slang word used for Vietnamese people.

GREEN BERETS – U.S. Special Forces soldiers.

GRUNT – Infantryman pulling time in the field.

GUNG HO – Totally military oriented.

GUNSHIP – Helicopters armed for support and battle purposes.

HOOTCH – Village living quarters for Vietnamese civilians.

HOT – The immediate area is under fire.

HUEY – Slang name for UH-1 helicopters.

HUMP – This is a term used by an infantryman when they are in the field walking with their equipment and weapons.

IN COUNTRY – On the soil of South Vietnam.

INSERT – When a unit is deployed into the field by helicopter.

K-BAR – Military issued combat survival knife.

KLICK – One kilometer.

LITTERS – Stretchers to carry wounded soldiers.

LIT-UP – Opened fire on.

M-16 – The standard small arms weapon issued to most American soldiers in Vietnam. Fired a 5.56mm round and replaced the M-14, due to lightweight.

M-60 – This was the standard issue lightweight machine gun issued to American units in Vietnam. Fired a 7.62mm round.

M-79 – Handheld grenade launcher used by American troops in Vietnam. Broke down like a shotgun. Fired a 40mm round that exploded on impact.

MEDEVAC – Helicopter used to evacuate wounded or killed soldiers from the field.

MINI-GUN – Machine gun with multiple barrels. Electronically operated and could fire 6,000 rounds per minute. Mounted in helicopters and other aircraft.

MORTAR – Weapon used to project a rocket style round long distances. Rounds explode on impact and project fragment pieces.

MP – Military police.

MPC – Military Payment Currency. Type of money that military personnel were issued in Vietnam.

NAPALM – A jelly substance that burns at a high temperature and is used against enemy forces. Usually dropped in the form of an exploding bomb from aircraft.

NVA – Members of the North Vietnamese Army. Usually well trained and well equipped.

PERIMETER – The extreme outer limitations of a military position.

POINT – The lead man in a combat patrol.

PUNJI STAKES – Sharpened bamboo sticks placed in hidden traps and used to mutilate or kill American soldiers.

PURPLE HEART – Award and decoration given to U.S. military personnel for wounds received by enemy action.

R & R – Rest and recreation.

RECON – Short for reconnaissance. Patrolling an area for enemy contact or observation.

ROCK N ROLL – Firing a weapon on fully automatic.

RPG – Short for rocket propelled grenade. Used effectively by the VC in heavy terrain combat or assaults on military positions.

SAPPER – An enemy soldier armed with explosives that successfully enter a fortified military stronghold.

SEARCH AND DESTROY – An operation where Americans search an area and destroy all enemy personnel, as well as their supplies.

SHORT – When a soldier's tour of duty is almost over.

SHORT-TIMER – A soldier nearing the completion of his Vietnam tour.

SHRAPNEL – Sharp and jagged pieces of metal propelled by an explosion. Meant to maim or kill enemy soldiers.

SKS – Semi-automatic rifle used by Vietnamese personnel. Fired a 7.62 round. Sometimes mounted with bayonet.

SLACK MAN – Second man in a patrol. Backup person for the point man.

SMOKE GRENADE – A grenade that produces a cloud of smoke. Used for signaling choppers and pinpointing unit location. Red always means danger.

SPECIAL FORCES – Green Beret soldiers.

STAND DOWN – When a unit completed a field mission and returned to a base camp for rest and re-supplies.

STARLIGHT SCOPE – A scope that intensifies night objects, by using light from the moon, stars and other light sources.

TRACER – An ammunition round that glows, due to a chemical treatment on its tip. Useful to help soldiers locate origin or destination of firing position.

USO – Short for United Service Organization. This group was in charge of entertainment for American troops stationed overseas. They were very active during the Vietnam War.

V – Style of ambush that was shaped like the letter.

VC – Slang for Viet Cong soldiers or sympathizers.

VIET CONG – Soldiers of the South Vietnamese Communist group.

WASTED – Killed.

WOOD LINE – The row of trees that borders an open area.

ZAPPED – Killed.

www.ingramcontent.com/pod-product-compliance
Lightning Source LLC
Chambersburg PA
CBHW041627140626
46547CB00031B/1169